Praise for
HOMER'S ODYSSEY

"A must-read for anyone who has ever loved an animal."
-Fredericksburg *Free Lance-Star*

"Heartwarming and entertaining."
-*People* Pets

"Delightful...This lovely human-feline memoir, following in the footsteps of Vicki Myron's best-selling *Dewey: The Small-Town Library Cat Who Touched the World,* is sure to warm the hearts of all pet lovers."
-*Library Journal* (starred review)

"A wonderful story celebrating the profound bond that can form between feline and human, *Homer's Odyssey* is an inspiring read, and a perfect holiday gift for any cat lovers on your list."
-*Feline Wellness*

"It took only a glance at the foreword, and before I knew it I was devouring the whole thing like a warm brownie sundae...It was Homer who most often proved to be the hero, once even saving Cooper's life when an intruder broke into her apartment. (This story alone is worth the price of the book.)"
-*The Christian Science Monitor*

BY GWEN COOPER

Homer's Odyssey

Love Saves the Day

GWEN COOPER

Homer

THE NINTH LIFE OF A
BLIND WONDER CAT

For Homer's Heroes--the men and women who work in rescue, the ones who adopt rather than shop, and those who know that when you help animals, you help people too. I never knew that writing about my cat would lead me to so many outstanding humans.

And for Laurence, always.

FOREWORD

I'VE BEEN WRESTLING WITH THE IDEA OF WRITING A SEQUEL TO *Homer's Odyssey* for nearly two years now—feeling, on the one hand, that there were certainly more Homer stories to be told; but, on the other hand, that to make something "book length" would require adding an awful lot of padding. *Homer's Odyssey* was published in 2009 and covered the first twelve years of Homer's life. Homer lived to be sixteen, and so a new book would have significantly less ground to cover.

What you are holding now is the solution I eventually reached—what I like to call a "mini-sequel," roughly one-third the length of the original. Not as long as many books, perhaps, but (I think) exactly the length it needs to be.

Length wasn't my only concern. I can't speak for other writers, but for me, to write about something is to relive it as vividly as I did the first time around. I don't know how to make a reader see and feel things that I'm not seeing and feeling myself at the moment I'm writing about them. There were many, many wonderful times with Homer during those four years after *Homer's Odyssey* came out, and you'll read those stories here. But there were also some hard times when we lost him, and I wasn't sure I could bear to go through them again.

Well, it wasn't the first time I've been wrong, and it won't be the last. One of the cruelest things about losing a loved one is the way that time makes our memories fade—until what remains isn't the substance of something, only the factual knowledge that it once existed. But, in writing this book, I've gotten to live with Homer again. I've gotten to feel his little head pushing hard into my hand as he demanded his daily pettings; to hear the distinctive *clip-clip* of his feet as he followed me down the hall; and to listen once more to the very specific melodic bird-song that ran beneath his purr. It's a sound I would instantly know from any other cat's purr, even if I were blindfolded.

The only thing that seems remarkable now is that I'd ever thought I was losing those things. And the only regret I have is that it's taken me so long to write my way back to them. I've spent the last weeks feeling Homer with me—the substance of him, a physical presence—as I haven't gotten to do in far too long.

That's the gift this book has given me. What I hope it will give to readers is more Homer, of course, more of the happy times they shared with us and loved in reading the first book, and all the comedy of seeing a little blind housecat—who, once upon a time, nobody else had wanted—take the world by storm.

I also hope that it will help bring clarity to some of the issues that we wrestled with—elder care and end-of-life issues that all animal guardians will have to face eventually. Medical treatment for animals has come a long way since I was a kid living in a family filled with rescue dogs. Often the question now isn't, *What* can *we do?* but, *What* should *we do?* How much money is too much to spend? How much aggressive medical care is justifiable, even if it's the only way to prolong a beloved cat's life?

There's no one right answer to these questions—although in this Foreword (and only in the Foreword), I'd like to float the idea of pet health insurance for anyone who knows they wouldn't be able to come up with, say, five thousand dollars in cash or credit at a moment's notice (which is probably most of us). The monthly premiums are very reasonable and, as they say, you can't put a price tag on peace of mind.

I was lucky as my cats grew older, in that whatever money I had, I'd earned by writing about *them*. I also didn't have children or a mortgage. So whether I could find the money for their care, and whether it was "prudent" to spend that money on them, weren't really questions. If the money came from them, then how could I not give it back?

Nevertheless, we ended up making very different decisions for Vashti, Scarlett, and Homer—because they were three very different cats. Vashti was easygoing and could handle whatever the doctors wanted to do, so we let them throw the whole arsenal at her. Scarlett was a surly girl and almost morbidly dignified, so we opted for a middle course—surgery for her cancer, but not chemotherapy or the removal (at the age of nearly seventeen) of her affected leg.

And Homer…well, Homer was Homer. He knew his own mind. He also knew his own strength—better, as it turned out, than even I did.

Certainly better than his doctors did.

And I have no doubt that when the kittens we adopted in 2012—whose antics, exploits, and hero-worship adoration of Homer you'll also read in these pages—become senior kitties someday, the decisions we make for them and with them will be different as well. Clayton and Fanny are as much one-of-a-kind individuals as our other cats ever were.

One last thought before moving on: Animals are luckier than humans, because animals get to live in the *now*. They do not fear death, or torment themselves with questions about what comes after. No cat has ever desperately hoped for one more year of life so she can finally see Paris, finish her memoirs, or watch her grandchildren graduate from high school. I genuinely believe that, if our animals could understand such things and talk to us about them, they wouldn't want us to spend ourselves into bankruptcy for the sake of trying to stretch fifteen years into sixteen, or even six years into twelve.

Cats know when they feel happy, when they feel comforted, and when they feel loved. None of us ever knows how much time we'll have, and you weren't put in your cat's life to guarantee him a certain minimum number of years. You were put in his life to provide him with happiness, comfort, and love. If you have given your cat (or dog, or bunny, or horse, or guinea pig) a life built on these things, then you've done your job, and you've done it perfectly.

And the moment you put all those things in jeopardy is the moment you'll know you've gone too far.

It will be hard to know these things in the chaos of that moment in which they're happening, when decisions have to be made. I know that firsthand. But if you pause for a moment, take a deep breath, and listen to your cat, he will tell you.

I've spent *far* more time discussing this here than I do in the book itself. First and foremost, this is a book of stories—stories about a cat who rose from obscurity to fame, who was promoted from barely tolerated baby brother to adored "big kid," and who continues to save the lives of other animals to this day, simply because *he* lived and his story was told.

Thank you for the gift of letting me tell these stories—and for the additional, greater gift of keeping Homer alive. As long as there is you, there will be him.

GWEN COOPER
New York, NY
November 26, 2015

CONTENTS

"Cat Lovers Don't Read Books"

There is no accounting for luck; Zeus gives prosperity to rich and poor just as he chooses, so you must take what he has seen fit to send you and make the best of it.

-HOMER, *The Odyssey*

FAMOUS CATS WEREN'T A *THING* LIKE THEY ARE TODAY, BACK WHEN I first began writing the proposal and outline for Homer's Odyssey in 2007. There were no cat cafes. Cat videos hadn't yet taken over the internet. The "Friskies 50" list of the internet's fifty most influential cats was years away not only from execution, but from any relevance. Everybody knew about famous animated cats, like Felix, Tom, Sylvester, the Aristocats, and the perennial Hello Kitty. I remembered a movie from childhood called That Darn Cat! There were celebrity cats like Morris and the elegant Fancy Feast Persian, although they were "played" by a succession of different cats, more brand icons than actual felines. A fictional kitty named Sneaky Pie

Brown starred in a series of cozy mystery novels. But there didn't seem to be any real-life famous cats, cats who were also members of real-life human families.

There was, however, a cat I'd read about in a recent newspaper article—a cat who'd lived in a library in small-town Iowa, and whose human caregiver had just sold a proposal for a book about his life for more than a million dollars.

My own first book, a novel about South Beach, had been published a few months earlier. Now I was trying to figure out a second book. I didn't think I could earn anything close to a million dollars for any book idea I might have, but I remember putting down the newspaper and looking across the living room at Homer—who was, at the time, visible only from the waist down, the upper half of his body buried under the sofa as he struggled to retrieve an intriguing new belled toy that had rolled away from him—and thinking, *I'll bet I could write a book about Homer. Homer's a pretty cool cat...*

Once I had the idea, I couldn't shake it loose—as if it had always been waiting there for me to unearth. Over the next few weeks, I started jotting down notes and writing out some preliminary paragraphs. I was still working full-time in an office, so I wrote in the pre-dawn hours of early morning—hours when Homer himself was the most active, sparking ideas and connections to half-forgotten memories of our earliest life together. Mornings were when Homer was likeliest to decide to use the toilet instead of the litter-box, to chase his big sisters down the hall (*Wait up, you guys!*), or to disrupt my writing with a preemptory head-bonk as he sat down smack in the middle of the computer keyboard, leaving me to wonder for the millionth time how a blind cat—just like any "normal" cat— infallibly *knew* when I was looking at a book or a newspaper or a computer screen, at anything rather than at him, and made up his mind to put an immediate end to *that.*

At the end of two months, I had enough written down to show my L.A.-based literary agent. He was decidedly underwhelmed by the whole thing. Those who've read the Afterword to the paperback edition of *Homer's Odyssey* may recall that his initial response was, "But why would anybody want to *read* this?"

"Because a lot of people like cats?" I'd been so flummoxed by his question that I heard myself phrasing my answer—a statement I knew for a fact to be true—as if it, too, were a question, the answer to which I was unsure of. "Because Homer is blind and interesting and has an inspirational life story?"

My agent was blunt. "The writing is there, but I don't think it's a good idea. I wouldn't be able to take it to editors."

I didn't just pay my agent to make deals for me—I also paid him for his career advice. He knew the publishing industry better than I did, and choosing to move forward with my blind-cat book against that advice was easier said than done.

I took to Google, trying to get a sense of how many others like me there might be out there—people who were also living with blind and "special-needs" cats. I ended up calling a woman named Alana Miller, who ran an organization called Blind Cat Rescue in North Carolina. We talked for a while about the plight of blind cats, the barriers they faced in finding adoptive homes, the way so many were summarily euthanized in open-intake shelters. We agreed—perhaps idealistically, but with utter sincerity—that if a book like this could save even one of them, it would be worth the effort of having written it.

I'd already been working with the notion of *blind leaps of faith* as being one of the central themes of this embryo book, and I decided to take one now. *Thank you so much for everything you've done for me, and for being the first person to have confidence in me as a writer,* I wrote to my agent a few days later. *But we see my proposed HOMER'S ODYSSEY project so very differently that I believe it's in our mutual best interests to part ways.*

I didn't know many other writers who could refer me to their agents, so I went back to what I had done to find my first one—

sending blind query letters and emails "over the transom" (meaning without a referral from another client). But this time I didn't have to wait close to a year to hear back, as I had with the first book. Within only a few weeks, a senior agent with a prestigious New York literary agency pronounced herself intrigued by both the writing and the story as I'd outlined it, despite being a self-professed "dog person." My confidence was bolstered by this—that I wasn't just getting the, *Awwwwww...Homer's a cute kitty!* endorsement—and also by how quickly I'd found an agent this time. Surely, I told myself, this could only auger good things. The two of us spent the next four or five months working together closely on an outline, a full proposal, and two sample chapters. We went back and forth over whether those sample chapters should simply be the first two chapters—or perhaps the story of Homer chasing off the burglar? Passages about Homer catching flies in mid-air? Homer and his Kleenex guitar? Final decisions were eventually made, and it was just after Memorial Day of 2008 when we decided we were ready to share *Homer's Odyssey*—at least in its broad strokes—with others.

It may have taken months to pull the proposal together, but it took only a few weeks for the rejections to start coming in from publishers. *The writing is wonderful, and I'd love to see more from this author,* the typical rejection would begin. *But in a crowded pet-memoir marketplace, I just don't feel that Homer is interesting enough to stand out.*

"Crowded marketplace?!" I'd exclaim to my agent. The only other cat memoir at the time was the one about Dewey, the Iowa library cat, and that hadn't even come out yet.

Ironically, Homer would usually be doing something that I thought was very interesting—or, at a minimum, entertaining—whenever one of these letters would come in. I remember that when I got the first one, Homer had just "liberated" a bag full of catnip toys I'd recently stocked up on. I'd double-wrapped the toys in two plastic bags, hidden those bags inside a duffle bag, and secreted the whole thing underneath a mound of clothes in the bottom of the closet, so that I could distribute them one at a time as the old ones wore out, without the cats' pestering me to death. But Homer's unerring nose had found them anyway. He'd burrowed assiduously into that mound of clothes intended for the laundry—kicking dirty socks and underwear into a heedless pile on the floor behind him—unzipped the duffel bag with his teeth and claws, and torn through the first plastic bag. Looking for all the world like Santa Claus (Santa Claws?), Homer now pranced down the hall and into the living room with the sack of toys between his teeth, the other  two cats for once following *him* eagerly as they waited for him to distribute the booty.

"Not *interesting* enough?!" Poor Laurence, then my husband-to-be, was generally the only receptacle for my indignation, which waxed hot when I'd receive one of these letters. *"The cat has no eyes!* Does he need to have no eyes and also learn how to juggle?" I'd demand. "Would that make them happy? Maybe if Homer had no eyes *and* could ask for his food in perfect sign language like Koko the gorilla."

That Homer wasn't "interesting" enough (or some variation of that) was what my agent and I heard most frequently. Also that animal lovers only wanted to read books about dogs and horses; that animal lovers didn't want to read animal books at all in "our current tech-centric environment;" that animal lovers were only receptive to picture books. One editor informed us matter-of-factly that "cat lovers don't read books." *Why do you think there aren't more cat books?* he asked with perfect *Catch-22* logic. Another said that, sure, maybe cat lovers read books, but they didn't read memoirs.

A third was confident that while cat lovers might read books—and while some of those books might even be memoirs—they definitely didn't read *cat* memoirs. (I wish I could say I was making this stuff up.)

By now, I had lost my job as a marketing executive at a magazine company, which had been acquired by another magazine company and then dissolved. The crux of my job had been the analysis of market research on our readers' consumer-spending habits. The "Marketing Analysis" section I'd written for the *Homer's Odyssey* proposal had been exhaustive. I'd provided data on the percentage of cat-owning U.S. households (roughly one third—or, expressed another way, around one hundred million Americans living with at least one cat); the amount of money spent per year by those households on cat-related products and services; and, specifically, the higher-than-average propensity of a wide swath of the U.S. cat-owning population to spend their disposable income on entertainment-related purchases, including dinners out, movie tickets, *and books*.

"If there's any hard data out there," I'd say to Laurence, "supporting the thesis that 'cat lovers don't read books,' I'd be pretty darn interested in seeing it." (I'm afraid I generally used a saltier word than *darn*. Forgive me. Those were dark days.)

At this point, our wedding was only a couple of months off, and I was starting to panic. It's all well and good to get married for richer or poorer, but it still feels awful to enter your marriage without a job or prospects or any viable means of earning an income. Homer was recovering from a recent health scare, the treatment of which had not only eaten into my finances, but had taken its emotional toll on us both. As much as I tried rationally to dismiss the idea, I had the persistent feeling that Homer had gotten sick *because* I wanted to write about him—that my hubris in thinking ours a story worth sharing publicly had been met by the powers that be with a not-so-gentle rebuke. I was supposed to cherish Homer as he was, the private heart of our own home, and be grateful for that.

It was when things seemed bleakest that I got an electrifying phone call from my agent. A large publishing imprint—one of the biggest and most venerable in the industry—was interested in *Homer's Odyssey*. Not only were they interested, they wanted to meet with me in person—along with my agent, a couple of senior editors, the group publisher, and various vice presidents in publicity and marketing. Then my agent said the words that every author dreams of hearing: "They're talking about a six-figure advance."

Six figures! Between my unemployed status and upcoming wedding, money was tight. Still, in the week I had before that meeting, I went out and bought a new outfit. I got my hair professionally blown out at a fancy SoHo salon. I invested in a forty-dollar manicure and sixty-dollar pedicure at a high-end spa in the Meatpacking District, rather than relying on the eight-dollar manicures I usually got from an elderly Chinese woman in our apartment building. (I was convinced that senior-level publishing muckety-mucks would be able to tell the difference.) I spent an hour carefully applying my makeup, so it would look like I wasn't wearing any. I even sprang for a hired car service to take me to the meeting, afraid of relying on the vagaries of afternoon cab availability to get me there on time.

I was already in the car and on my way uptown when I got the call from my agent. Everything had been cancelled. The group publisher (the big boss, basically) hadn't known what the book was about until shortly before the meeting was supposed to begin. She'd never heard of anything as "creepy" as a cat without eyes, and she was appalled that anyone on her team had considered acquiring *Homer's Odyssey*. There was a rumor afloat that she'd gone so far as demoting the senior editor who'd first read the proposal and recommended it for acquisition—as an example to others never to let anything this awful cross her desk again.

"*Homer's Odyssey* now has an official body count," I told

Laurence grimly that night, when he got home from work and asked how my meeting had gone.

I'm not sure which hurt worse—the brutality of that last-minute cancellation, after a week of raised hopes and what now seemed like a pathetic level of over-preparation. Or hearing poor Homer, tiny Homer who'd never done a mean thing to anyone in his life, described as "creepy."

And whose fault is that? I asked myself. Who had subjected Homer to the mockery and derision of ignorant strangers?

I had. I had done it. And even though I knew Homer had no idea that anything unkind had been said about him—or even that such a thing as unkind words existed—those words had opened a wound right in my heart. It hadn't taken much to revive fears I'd had years ago—the sense that it was my job to safeguard Homer in the disability I'd long-since stopped thinking of that way, to protect him against people who wouldn't understand him, or who would say ugly things merely because he was different.

Homer didn't know why he, along with Scarlett and Vashti, unexpectedly found tuna mixed in with their dinner that night. He didn't know why I cuddled him closer on the couch before going to bed. He merely purred with contentment, nuzzling his head into the crook of my neck as he drifted off to sleep.

Technically, this hadn't been the final word. There were still a few more editors we hadn't heard back from. It was possible that one of them might decide to give *Homer's Odyssey* a shot.

But I knew I was finished with the whole business. It was one thing to take a blind leap of faith. It was quite another to bang your head—your own and the heads of the ones you loved—repeatedly against the same brick wall, with nothing to show for it but lumps. As soon as I returned from my honeymoon, I vowed, I would send out résumés and look for a proper job.

I got married two weeks later, and drifted through my wedding day as serene as if everything had already been settled. As far as I was concerned, it had.

LAURENCE AND I were married on September 13, 2008, and left for our honeymoon the next evening. And while we spent the following week lolling on Bahamian beaches, enjoying those first few days of married life, the world fell apart.

We returned to find that what would eventually be called the Great Recession had kicked off in our absence. The job I'd been sure I would land, once I devoted my time to looking, now seemed a dubious proposition at best. Nobody was hiring.

So, when I got an email from my agent a week after our return, I saw things in a much different light than I had right before the wedding. An editor named Caitlin Alexander at Delacorte, a Random House imprint, wanted to acquire *Homer's Odyssey.* After a few days of back-and-forth with my agent over numbers, they made us an offer—not the million-plus dollars the book about Dewey had sold for, but enough to cover my rent and, if I was thrifty, basic living expenses for a year. Even better than the money was Caitlin herself—kind and cat-loving but also sharp, with ideas for improving my outline that were so insightful, I was excited at the prospect of working with her.

It was Homer who gave Caitlin the final seal of approval, the night she came to our apartment for dinner. "So this is *Homer*," she said, when Homer made his usual appearance at the front door to greet the new person. There was a kind of reverence in the way she said his name, a tone that previously Homer had only been used to hearing in *my* voice, and he responded to it immediately. Caitlin crouched down and placed one of her hands beneath his nose for him to sniff. But Homer was far more interested in the cat treats she'd brought and now held in the other. One paw reached up delicately to swipe them onto the floor, where he greedily gobbled them up. Once all the treats had been dispatched, Homer placed both front paws on Caitlin's knee, so he could raise himself up and sniff her more thoroughly—obviously hoping for more treats. Caitlin was enraptured, answering Laurence and me in an absent-minded way when we spoke, wholly preoccupied with watching Homer.

"Would you like a glass of wine, Caitlin?" I asked.

"Hmmm…?" Caitlin was scratching Homer beneath his chin, fascinated with watching the muscles around the place where his eyes would have been relax in pleasure. "Sure, that sounds good."

"Red or white?"

Homer had now flopped onto the floor and rolled halfway onto his back, delighted with the attention as Caitlin continued to stroke his chin and neck. "Oh…whichever. Hey, look how well he gets around!" she exclaimed, as Homer—deciding he'd received enough pettings for now, and realizing that no further treats were immediately forthcoming—walked off to find something more entertaining to do. "Look how he knows exactly where his toys are! And he doesn't bump into anything!"

Scarlett and Vashti observed all this from the sidelines with a kind of harrumph-y disdain. *What's so interesting?* they seemed to be asking themselves. *It's just* Homer, *for crying out loud. We manage not to bump into things all the time.*

Although we didn't know it at the time, this would become a sort of template for the way many encounters would play out in our home over the next year.

The paperwork for *Homer's Odyssey* was finalized in late October of 2008, and the book was scheduled for publication in late August of 2009. It seemed a long way off. But to make that publication date, I would have to write the entire book by the end of January. I buckled down, and by working fifteen-hour days I managed to have my complete first draft written and submitted by Monday, February 2.

Homer would have his first professional photo shoot later that same day.

By then, the book about Dewey the Library Cat had finally

"pubbed," and it had been a big hit. Suddenly, the conventional wisdom on whether or not there was a market for cat memoirs had shifted. Between that and the success of *Marley and Me,* pet memoirs were the hot new thing. And what had begun as the small passion project of one cat-loving editor had now become worthy of the full weight of Delacorte's serious attention.

I had taken numerous photos of Homer when I'd first started working on the book proposal, in order to submit them along with the writing. They had been deemed "just darling" by Caitlin, although of course none of them were of the professional caliber required to grace the cover of a book Delacorte hoped might be one of its bigger Fall '09 titles. A professional photographer was therefore dispatched to our apartment with all due haste—and an entirely new phase in our lives began.

People who came to see us had always been interested in Homer. He was (the opinion of certain editors notwithstanding) an interesting little guy. But now began an influx of visitors who were *only* interested in Homer. My day would come eventually, further down the road, when it was time to do in-studio radio spots or phone interviews for newspapers and magazines. I was fated to become one of the luckiest "cat ladies" ever—because people *wanted* to hear me talk about my cat! At length! Sometimes for as long as an hour at a stretch!

The focus for now, however, was on turning Homer into a star. You've probably heard that stars aren't born, they're made. Well, I'm here to tell you that it's true. Behind every star is an entire team of people invisible to the public. Not just the photographers, the editors, the lighting assistants, the stylists (or, in the case of a cat, professional groomers—although they learned quickly that *our* star strongly preferred *not* to have anyone but mom trim his claws or touch his paws, thank you very much). There are also managers, publicists, "stage moms," personal assistants, gatekeepers, and lackeys whose job it is to keep the star happy and engaged, to get him out of his trailer in time for the shoot and in a suitable emotional state to work, to run and fetch whatever the star may want to eat or amuse himself with.

When it came to making Homer a star, all of those latter roles were filled by me—with an occasional assist from Laurence, who these days was working from home. (The L.A.-based entertainment magazine where he was an editor hadn't laid off staff yet, but they had sent their Manhattan-based employees to work at home, so they could liquidate their New York office—which we took to be an ominous sign.) Laurence, however, would usually clear out for the day whenever our apartment was taken over for video or photo shoots.

"Managing" Homer soon became my full-time job. It was my responsibility to set his appointments; thoroughly brush and groom him ahead of time, so that his coat would shine with a high gloss and without any pesky stray bits of fur that might dangle from his haunches and ruin a shot; to make sure he got plenty of rest before a shoot began; to keep us stocked up on the tuna, turkey, and toys required to keep him engaged, happy, and playful; to wrangle him from spot to spot as the daylight or whims of whoever was shooting him changed.

I had to pop open cans of tuna when they wanted Homer to raise his head and perk up his ears; to dip toys and crumpled pieces of paper and bits of sisal rope in the tuna oil when Homer's interest in them flagged and he'd start to trot over to me. *Why aren't you playing with any of this cool stuff, mom?* I had to gauge when it was finally time for Homer to retire to the sanctity of his cat tree for a quick, replenishing cat nap. I'd gently suggest to whoever was in charge that Homer really *could* use a bit of time to himself— at which point he or she would cry, "That's lunch, everybody!" and the cameramen, the sound crew (if it was a video shoot), the lighting techs, the groomer and stylist, the field producer, and the field producer's assistant would ask me to recommend a nearby restaurant. And would I mind terribly calling ahead for a reservation, since they'd need a large table?

It was my job to do all these things and more and then...to get out of the shot.

I used to joke that my name might as well officially be changed to Gwen "Thank You Now Please Get Out Of The Shot" Cooper. "We'd like to shoot Homer in front of the bookcase—he looks adorable with all those books behind him! Thank you so much [after I'd lured Homer to the desired spot with a cheerful, *Come on, Homer-Bear!*]...but could you move juuuuuuust a little to the left? A little more? We can still see part of your arm."

Or, "I'd like to get Homer in front of the window. He'll be majestic with the Manhattan skyline behind him. Could you get him to...yes...perfect, that's it! But your hair is so curly and it's interfering with Homer's light—could you maybe pull it back?"

Far be it for me to interfere with Homer's light!

If Homer had been a different kind of a cat—a cat like Scarlett, for example—all the "managing" in the world couldn't have made these shoots possible. But Homer had always liked attention, and the people who gave it to him. He was intriguing not just because of his blindness, but because he had real charisma.

That might sound like an odd word to apply to a cat. Charisma, though, is little more than the ability of some people (or cats) to make you feel—even if only for the span of a few minutes—as if *you* are the most fascinating thing going, the very person they'd been hoping to get to spend time with.

Homer had that ability in spades.

Every strange person who came to our home and crawled on their belly holding a camera before them—so as to shoot Homer at his own level—was one more friend for him to make, one more cheerful greeting for him to bestow, receiving a playful scratch behind his ears in return. Scarlett and Vashti ran for the hills whenever our apartment was thus inundated, but Homer could never get over how much cool *stuff* these people brought with them! Cartons and crates, lighting reflectors, boom mics, duffel bags for Homer to crawl in, around, and over. His nose and whiskers would twitch non-stop as he tried to process all the exotic new smells of equipment bags that had been on airplanes, in studios and out on location shoots, perhaps even (in the case of the crew from Animal Planet) in the homes of other cats.

Homer resting in his "trailer" between takes

The camera crews came to our home as a team of seen-it-all professionals, out on just another job—and an annoying one at that, because what could be more irritating (or less interesting) than working with a *cat*?—but they left as an adoring cult. Like my former boyfriends of old, who'd proudly proclaimed, *Homer's my buddy!*, each photographer and videographer was convinced that he or she had formed a unique and special bond with Homer over the course of the shoot, that some magical *thing* had happened between the two of them during those few hours they had together.

Homer could make you feel that way. He seemed to know precisely when they wanted him to sit still as a statue and look majestic, to chase around toys in goofy, kittenish fashion, to run or jump or flip around on his back with un-self-conscious abandon, to turn his head shyly a little to the side, as if to say, *I'm strong, but also vulnerable.* Maybe he even *did* know. Homer was a sensitive cat, one who'd always paid close attention to the people around him. He had ways of knowing things that even I couldn't account for.

Do you see this?, they'd demand. *Do you see how he's responding to me?* Click-click, the camera would go. *He's a great cat, Gwen, a really exceptional cat.* And then they'd remind me, for the umpteenth time to, please, get out of the shot.

I knew that I hovered. Part of it was my old over-protectiveness, which reared up again and was hard to suppress as I watched strangers cluster around Homer, amidst walls of gear five times his size. As for Homer himself, he was almost never nervous with all the activity going on around him. All he needed to find these unprecedented new experiences completely enjoyable was the knowledge that I was somewhere nearby. But with so much going on—with so many people and so much equipment crammed within the relatively small space of our living room—it was difficult for him to catch my scent if I wasn't standing close. Speaking to him in a reassuring voice wasn't a great option, as it tended to cause him to leave off whatever he'd been doing and head in my direction.

As soon as Homer wasn't sure I was there anymore—when the horrifying thought that I might have left him *alone* with all these strangers appeared to cross his mind—then he was capable of being as uncooperative as any irate star. The fur on his back would start to rise, he'd twist his head wildly in un-shoot-able postures, nose in the air as he tried to figure out my location. I'd rush over to pet him and smooth down his fur. *I'm not going anywhere, Homer-Bear. I'm right here with you.* Thus calmed and restored to cheerful good humor, Homer would once again return to the work at hand as if he'd been born to do it.

And I, of course, would hasten to get out of the shot.

ALL TOLD, THERE were only perhaps seven or eight of these shoots, stretched out over nearly as many months. But they loomed so large with their strangeness and excitement that they cast long shadows. As the count-down to *Homer's Odyssey*'s publication date began, and as the anxiety and anticipation continued to build, it was hard to feel that our lives were quite what they had been only a few months ago—although it was equally hard to say just what, exactly, they were becoming.

Some of these shoots were arranged by my publisher for their own purposes—two sessions in our home in order to get the ideal cover shot of Homer (as well as extras to be used inside the book itself), and one at an off-site photographer's studio for additional publicity shots of Homer and me together. I talked about that one in the Afterword for *Homer's Odyssey*—the near impossibility of wrangling Homer in an unfamiliar space, trying to get him to stay still long enough to have his picture taken. All Homer himself wanted to do was explore this new place and introduce himself to all the new people within it. It was so *very* hard to get him to sit

© Jessica Hills Photography

still that, as I noted in the Afterword, eventually the photographer and lighting techs unhooked all the equipment from its various stands and carried it by hand, so they could follow Homer wherever he went. As long as I live, I'll never forget the sight of a team of professionals—and one hovering stage mom—following along behind a blind cat in parade-like fashion, crying, *Wait! I think he's going* this *way now!*

People magazine wanted photos of Homer for insets to accompany the full-page review of the book they planned to run. *Ladies Home Journal* was going to excerpt a portion of *Homer's Odyssey*—from the chapter describing the night Homer had chased off the burglar—in their September issue. For this shoot, along with the usual crew they also sent over to our apartment a hair-and-make-up person and wardrobe stylist for me. They wanted shots of Homer and me together to accompany the piece—shots of Homer lying on my chest, shots of Homer in my arms, shots of Homer nuzzling my ear. In the end, though, they ran a photo of just Homer by himself.

"The problem," as I would later observe to a friend, when the issue came out and I saw that I wasn't in it, "is that I didn't get out of the shot."

Animal Planet did a segment on Homer for their *Cats 101* show. The segment was only a few minutes long, but it took a grueling eight hours to get all the footage they needed. Even Homer was spent by the end of the day, when our apartment was in shambles and all he wanted was to use his litter-box without having a cameraman closely following his movements. At one point, he turned with an indignant hiss on the cameraman, who followed behind him with dogged persistence. *Do you mind? I'm trying to pee in privacy!* I will say, though, that nobody we worked with knew how to record cats more unobtrusively than the Animal Planet crew. They were even able to capture the notoriously camera-shy Vashti and Scarlett, and there was no way any of us would have made it through a day that long without their expertise.

The coverage for *USA Today* happened in three waves. The books editor—the person who decided which books *USA Today* would cover; which of their various staff and freelance reviewers would be assigned to cover them; and who also wrote the revered-within-the-industry "Book Buzz" column, which a month earlier had decreed that, *"Homer's Odyssey* will be huge," causing bookstore pre-orders to quintuple overnight—was also a cat lover. ("So much for cat lovers not reading books," I told my agent.). She wanted to do more with *Homer's Odyssey* than simply have it reviewed, and she came over to our apartment to interview me personally— although I didn't kid myself that so high-ranking a personage would have gone to all the trouble of coming to me if she hadn't wanted to meet Homer as well.

Homer seemed almost relieved when someone came to our home wanting only to sit and chat, rather than putting him through his paces. He curled up in my lap for most of the interview, drowsy and comfortable as the editor reached out from time to time to stroke his head. "He really is a loving little guy, isn't he," she observed, and Homer rewarded this by pushing his entire face into her hand, his way of demanding that she rub him harder. For once, even Scarlett and Vashti ventured out, eager to feast upon the cat treats I'd scattered around liberally as a way of ensuring that Homer would stay in the living room throughout the interview and not head off to his "trailer"—i.e. the little cave in his cat tree. Homer, however, was more interested in the editor than in the treats, having had so many in recent weeks that he was becoming ever-so-slightly bored with them. (Ah, the ennui of stardom!)

A day later, a photographer from *USA Today* came to shoot Homer for the story—one lone photo-journalist and his camera, without all the rigging and light reflectors and duffle bags we'd become accustomed to. I was so used to being asked to...you know...get out of the shot that I was wearing work clothes, the hair I'd washed but hadn't bothered styling that morning (because who cared what *I* looked like?) pulled back in an untidy ponytail. But the books editor had instructed the photographer to shoot Homer and me together—which is why, to my everlasting shame, Homer and I were immortalized in the pages of the nation's biggest newspaper with me looking like I'd just finished moving furniture.

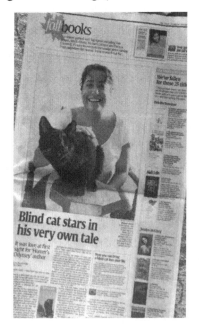

Homer, it goes without saying, looked sleek and shiny and impossibly perfect.

The day after *that*, a *USA Today* videographer arrived to film me reading an excerpt of *Homer's Odyssey* while Homer scampered in the background, planning to post the video to the *USA Today* website and YouTube channel once the book had been released. I'd invested in a brand-new catnip toy for the occasion, in order to ensure maximum frolicking. Homer systematically demolished that toy over the course of the hour it took us to shoot, tearing it to shreds and releasing all the catnip into a giant mound in front of him, which he then rolled and flipped around in while his entire face became encrusted with 'nip—until he looked like Al Pacino at the end of *Scarface*. The catnip made Homer talkative, and so that footage is one of the very few recordings in existence that captured the sound of Homer's own voice—and, for that reason, I treasure it to this day.

Perhaps the craziest day was when we recorded the book trailer—the promotional video commissioned by my publisher for placement on YouTube and various other websites. They'd taken over a two-bedroom suite at the Hotel Pennsylvania for the shoot, across the street from Madison Square Garden, where many a visiting rocker had stayed and partied back in the hotel's glory days.

They sent a town car to pick Homer and me up. Homer had been reluctant to get into his carrier, and it was raining as I dashed as quickly as I could from apartment building to car—although Homer did catch a few drops, which didn't improve his mood. The driver helped me load in all the gear I'd thought necessary to bring along if we were going to be shooting out of the house for an entire day—a litter-box and litter, bowls for food and water and food to go in them, a sack of catnip, a bag of Pounce treats, and a large bag of rolling-and-belled toys. I was scheduled for an early-morning arrival—before seven—and I'd requested that as few people as necessary be there when we first arrived, so that Homer would have time to acclimate to a new place before it was time for the hair-and-makeup person to go to work on me, and the groomer to go to work on him.

There was a single cameraman there to greet us when we knocked on the door of the suite. He'd beaten us to the hotel by only an hour, having just arrived on a red-eye from L.A. for the purpose of recording Homer's first hour of exploration. I set up food and water bowls for Homer in the kitchen, and placed the litter-box there as well, setting Homer in the litter-box first—as was our custom when I brought him to a new place—so that he wouldn't have to wonder where it was.

"I've never seen such big aural canals in a cat," the cameraman noted. "You can see all the way down into his ears. They're huge!"

"Homer's hearing is off the charts," I agreed, as Homer's head perked up at the sound of my saying his name, and he turned the ears we'd just been discussing in my direction.

"Are you sure he's never been here before?" The cameraman was watching as Homer—nose to the ground—began to figure out the suite and its various rooms. He didn't bump into a single thing, not a wall, not a sofa, not the cabinets in the kitchen or a lamp in the suite's living room. Homer's sensitive nose and remarkable whiskers gave him all the information he needed to navigate seamlessly—just as he'd done time after time in the many homes we'd moved in and out of, back in our earlier years of struggle and constant migration. After about a half-hour of thorough investigation, Homer happily took up play with a catnip ball, fascinated with the way it ricocheted off the bottom of the kitchen cabinets and into the living room. He chased it in and out of bedrooms, under tables, around the sofa and floor lamps, without losing track of it for even a moment.

"I can't believe he's *blind*," the cameraman marveled. "Don't take this the wrong way, but if it weren't for the fact that his eyes are gone, I'd say you were lying."

I laughed. "My husband says the same thing," I told him. "To this day, he swears that Homer's faking blindness."

It was a long day, and the suite began to fill up as the morning wore on. The next to arrive were Homer's and my respective groomers, followed by another cameraman, a lighting tech with trees and enormous reflective panels ("It's hard to get the lighting just right on a black cat," he explained—which I already knew), a sound person with boom mics, a producer, Caitlin, and my publisher's Vice President of Marketing, who had arrived to supervise the shoot personally.

But, with all the primping and preparation, with all the setting up of equipment and moving of furniture, with all the phone calls and consultations and last-minute disagreements about the shot list (which detailed the specific things they wanted to capture Homer doing), it was hours before the shoot proper—wherein I would answer questions about Homer and the book, while Homer did various adorable and active things in the background—even started.

By then, as was his preferred habit on rainy days when thunder rolled with a pleasant far-away rumble beneath the sounds of drops splashing against the windows, Homer wasn't interested in doing anything but napping. He wasn't upset. He was friendly as ever when new people came over to greet him and introduce themselves. He was simply *bored.* All the hoopla over the last few months, all the duffel bags and equipment and strangers and cat treats, all the new toys and the cameras following him to catch his every movement as he sat or ran or stretched or jumped or rolled over, had become old hat. All Homer wanted to do now was sit quietly on the couch behind my head, the way we did on rainy days when we were home alone and I read a book while Homer snoozed peacefully beside me.

Everybody's eyes were on me. But, as every cat person knows, there's only so much you can do with an uncooperative cat. I tried opening a baggie of catnip and wafting it under his nose. Nothing. I tried jangling a belled toy next to his ear. No response.

I got up and walked across the room. "Homer," I cooed. "Homer, come over to mommy."

Homer flicked one ear lazily in the direction of my voice, but didn't stir. *Nah,* he seemed to say. *Don't wanna.*

"Homer-Bear," I sing-songed. I tried rattling a bag of

Pounces. "Do you want a treat, Homer? Do you want to come and get a kitty treat, baby boy?"

Homer yawned mightily and extended his front and hind legs in a long, languorous stretch. He flipped onto his back momentarily, then curled back into a ball and continued to nap.

And so, here we were. A room full of people, a crew of professionals who'd flown through the night all the way from the West Coast, my publisher's Vice President of Marketing (upon whom, I couldn't help but feel, I was making a very bad impression), all the treats and toys any cat would want—all of it here for Homer, and *only* for Homer, and Homer himself couldn't be bothered. He'd already been there. He'd already done that.

"Let me make a call," I told the room, and went to dig my cell out of my purse so I could phone Laurence at home.

"I need you," I told him as soon as he answered. "We need half a pound of that sliced deli turkey Homer likes, and a whole bunch of those little cans of tuna. Do you think you could go to the grocery store and then bring it all here?"

"Yeah, sure." Laurence sounded surprised, but willing to help. "What do you want, Chicken of the Sea?"

"No, no." I was beginning to sound frantic. "Not Chicken of the Sea! He likes Bumble Bee, Laurence. *Homer likes Bumble Bee!*"

There was a pause, and then we both began to laugh. We laughed until we were practically crying. Tears ran down my face and my stomach began to ache, making it hard to breathe as I tried to suppress the laughter, aware that all the people in the other room could probably hear me.

Our lives *had* gotten a little crazy. But Homer wasn't some diva, and we weren't his flunkies. Homer was still just *Homer*—the good-natured, high-spirited little boy we fondled and fussed over at home, in private, as soon as the cameras were packed up and gone.

I'd been making myself crazy in part because—yes—I

desperately wanted my book to be a success. What author doesn't want that? I knew how incredibly rare it was for a publisher to put this kind of effort and attention into a book, that this particular moment in my life was fleeting and one I needed to enjoy as it was happening, because Homer and I wouldn't be the flavor of the month forever.

But it was more than that. I was also *proud* of Homer—not just of the ease and dignity with which he'd been acquitting himself as all these unusual and unprecedented things were happening to us. I was proud of who he was. I felt entirely vindicated in all the years of faith I'd had in him. And I wanted others to see that. I wanted the whole world to see—naysayers I'd never even met and probably never would, who nevertheless I knew would think, *Why would anybody want a blind cat?* I wanted everybody to view for themselves what a blind cat—*my* blind cat—could do. The veterinarian from whom I'd adopted Homer was writing the Foreword to *Homer's Odyssey*, and I had an idea that some of the people who'd had the chance to adopt him but turned him down, all those years ago, might read this book. They might put two and two together, they might realize what they had discarded as if it were nothing. Their loss had been my infinite gain, but still I wanted them to view Homer with amazement, to read his story with envy and think, *That could have been me.*

And, although I generally didn't consider myself a vindictive person, I wanted to make that one publisher who'd called Homer "creepy" eat her words. I wanted to make her rue the day she'd turned from him in disgust. *I'll show you "creepy,"* I'd say to myself, in steely tones.

Before any of that would happen, however, there was still our immediate problem to contend with—a cat already bored with a fame he technically hadn't attained yet, and the necessity of recapturing his interest just long enough to make it through this last shoot.

"I'll be there as soon as I can with turkey and tuna," Laurence promised, when we had finished laughing.

"Thank you," I told him. "Oh—and make sure it's the fancy albacore. That's his favorite."

Laurence ran out to the grocery store in the rain, waited forever to find a cab—which was always tougher on soggy days like this—and sat in the heavy crosstown traffic for nearly half an hour as he crossed from Second Avenue to where we were waiting at the Hotel Pennsylvania on Seventh. Once he arrived, we had to open a slew of those little cans of tuna before the sound of cans opening and the aroma of fish filling the room intrigued Homer enough to rouse him from his slumber. Laurence went into the suite's kitchen and rattled the paper Homer's favorite turkey was wrapped in, actually going through the motions of making a sandwich until Homer rose languidly from the sofa and trotted into the kitchen to paw at Laurence's leg. *Hey—is that turkey?*

The shoot ran longer than scheduled, but in the end we got the footage of Homer we needed. I took a look at the demolished suite as I was packing up Homer and his gear to head back home. Furniture had been pushed around haphazardly. Lampshades were skewed at odd angles, positioned this way and that to better cast the light onto Homer's black fur. Cameras and lighting reflectors were lying on the floor or leaned against end tables. Nearly two dozen small, half-opened cans of tuna were scattered on every imaginable surface, along with uneaten bits of turkey strewn across the floor, laid there to tempt Homer into various spots. The whole space was torn apart, as if a herd of wild animals had stampeded their way through.

I shook my head in amazement as I took it all in, thinking, *Well, I guess we've finally arrived.* Homer had trashed his first hotel room. He was officially a star.

The World's Cat

**The Muse brought to the minstrel's mind a song of
heroes whose great fame rang under heaven.**

-HOMER, *The Odyssey*

HOMER'S ODYSSEY WAS PUBLISHED ON AUGUST 25, 2009. I HAD
traveled to Washington, D.C. the night before to do an interview on
NPR's "Diane Rehm Show" on the morning of launch, and didn't
get back home again until the early evening. Homer spent the
night of the book's release feasting on the lobster salad Laurence
had prepared for me as a congratulatory surprise, but that I was too
wound-up to eat. Scarlett and Vashti didn't care as much for lobster,
but Laurence had bought them a tin of fancy canned tuna from our
local gourmet shop—which Homer consumed his fair share of as
well. I spent the rest of the night refreshing the book's Amazon
page every hour, so I could watch as its sales rank rose. (This is
something every writer does on the day her book is published, and

any writer who tells you she doesn't is totally lying.) Eventually, I moved my laptop computer over to the couch, so I wouldn't have to keep jumping up to see if the numbers had changed. Homer, full of lobster and tuna, snoozed happily beside me.

With all the pre-publication craziness, I'd thought that life would calm down once the book was out. But, soon after it appeared in bookstores, there came a second, smaller wave of press rolling through our apartment in order to meet Homer—the bloggers, vloggers (those with video blogs), and internet radio hosts who hadn't required the longer lead times of magazines and newspapers, and who were thus able to wait until the book was on shelves before planning their coverage.

This second wave of press was much mellower than the first had been, requiring far less of Homer and me. Usually it would just be one person with a hand-held recording device, or perhaps one additional person to hold a video camera. Homer was able to interact with these people with nothing more than his usual level of friendly interest—although I do remember one blogger in particular for whom Homer went absolutely wild.

I had never been nearly as aware of different people's differing smells as Homer was, but this specific blogger had an especially… pungent…aroma that even I could catch from across the room. She smelled strongly of patchouli mixed with insufficiently masked body odor—which is really only worth mentioning because Homer was fascinated by this woman as he'd never been with anyone before, and as I would never see him be with anyone again. It was impossible to keep him off her, to prevent him from crawling up and around her as he tried to take in her scent from all conceivable angles, burying his head in her hair and inserting his nose deeply into more private areas.

"He's certainly a friendly little guy, isn't he?" the blogger observed, trying to angle Homer's nose unobtrusively away from her crotch.

"That he is." I was mortified. "Homer! *Homer! Come...
here!*" I spoke in the guttural-voice-through-clenched-teeth tone my
own mother had used to rein me in when I was small, whenever
my childish high spirits had seemed in danger of causing public
embarrassment.

Homer, however, was not to be deterred. "I'm *so* sorry," I
apologized. "I don't know what's come over him." Homer's head
was still immersed in our guest's nether regions, and finally I went
over and lifted him from her, one hand under his breastbone for
support while the other took the scruff of his neck in a manner meant
to indicate, *I am NOT kidding around!*

But Homer wriggled out of my arms and boomeranged
right back to his intrusive examination of every square inch of the
blogger's body. "I can put him in the other room, if you'd like," I
offered.

"No, don't worry about it!" I may have been appalled at
Homer's bad behavior, but the blogger herself seemed unruffled.
"But maybe we should open a window?" she added. "Your face
looks a little red."

Of all the people who came and went through our home,
convinced that during their time with us they'd formed a special
bond with Homer unlike anybody else's, this was the one occasion
when that was likeliest to be true.

There were perhaps a half-dozen or so of these visitors over
the course of a couple of days, and then Laurence and I hit the road.
Publishers weren't as apt to finance book tours as they'd been once
upon a time, but I scheduled a few readings on my own. I did one
in New York, of course, where we lived. I did one in L.A. where,
after nearly two decades as a film journalist, Laurence had many
friends. And I scheduled one in Miami where my parents and some
of my old friends still lived. Laurence had given me a necklace to
celebrate the book's publication, featuring a tiny cat-shaped pendant
made from small black diamonds, and I wore it for luck whenever I

made a book-related appearance.

In Miami, I did an in-studio interview at the local NPR station the morning before my reading, and an article about the book and my upcoming appearance was published in the *Miami Herald* the same day. Still, I wasn't expecting much of a turnout beyond my family, my friends, and my parents' friends. Part of the reason why publishers were reluctant to underwrite book tours was because it had become increasingly difficult to get people to turn out for them, even when a book was popular and an author event had been well publicized.

So it was overwhelming to arrive at Books & Books in Coral Gables and find that nearly three hundred people had come. *Three hundred people!* The lead book reviewer for the *Sun-Sentinel*, whose work I'd been reading since I was a teenager, was the one who stepped up to the podium to introduce me, and it was one of the great nights of my life.

I don't think it really hit me until that moment that a *lot* of people were going to read Homer's story. It was one thing to see sales figures projected on a spread sheet, but an entirely different experience to see three hundred individual faces turned my way as I read from the book. There was even a cat in attendance—a tiny blind kitten named Galileo, only a few weeks old, with the two people who'd found him abandoned a few days earlier. They'd brought Galileo to the reading in the hopes that somebody there might be able to help them figure out what to do for him—and, sure enough, representatives from several local rescue groups were on-hand and able to take charge of the situation. (Galileo eventually found a forever home with a reader in Ft. Lauderdale.)

I also realized something else that night that I'd never thought about before—the deep chord that *Homer's Odyssey* would strike in the animal-rescue community. Homer represented any number of cats who rescuers would cry themselves to sleep at night thinking about—cats who were sweet and friendly and loving, cats these rescuers worked with every day, and who they knew would make a wonderful companion to anyone lucky enough to adopt them. But cats (and dogs) who, nevertheless, were consistently passed over for adoption because they were blind, or deaf, or needed extra care for ongoing medical issues, or simply because they had aged out of kitten-hood and were now "too old."

I wasn't the only one who stood vindicated by the publication of Homer's story. And, despite having cared for him for more than twelve years, I wasn't even close to being the one who'd put in the most time and effort—who'd fought the most battles or broken her heart the most often—trying to prove that a special-needs animal was just as capable of loving and being loved as any other, and just as deserving of a chance.

Eight days after *Homer's Odyssey* was published, I received two phone calls—one from Caitlin, and one from the in-house publicist my publisher had assigned to promote *Homer's Odyssey*, both with the same exciting news. After only one week on sale, *Homer's Odyssey* would debut at #14 on the following week's *New York Times* Bestseller List.

Laurence and I celebrated with champagne that night, while Homer, Vashti, and Scarlett were treated to new catnip toys and Homer's beloved deli turkey. When the *New York Times* Book Review in which Homer would be named was finally published, I saw that *Homer's Odyssey* had been called out for special attention in the "Inside the List" feature that ran alongside it. "*Homer's Odyssey* makes its first appearance on the list in 2,720 years," the writer humorously observed, before adding, "Oh, wait! Gwen Cooper's book is actually the story of a tiny blind wonder cat..."

THE NEXT FEW months were a whirlwind. Although I hadn't been sent on an official book tour, I was invited to speak at shelters and at shelter fundraisers around the country, to advocate for the cause of special-needs animals and of rescue in general.

I hated leaving my three cats as often as I did, traveling more now than I had at any previous time in my life. But, then, I was now firmly self-employed, so when I was home I got to be *home*. My cats and I had never had so many uninterrupted hours in the day together as we did during the times when I wasn't on the road. Homer would greet me with pure delight when I returned from a trip—happy I was back, of course, and also eager to make a thorough investigation of my suitcase and my person. Every engagement I traveled to included a tour through the shelter where I'd be speaking, along with plenty of cuddling opportunities with the cats that shelter cared for. No matter how thoroughly I showered before getting on a plane, the shoes I wore home and the bag containing clothing I'd worn while away reeked, from Homer's perspective, of other cats. It could take hours for Homer to get through as exhaustive an inspection as he liked, until finally it was time to dump my suitcase contents into the laundry and get them ready for the next trip.

Best of all were the gifts I brought back for the cats. Everywhere I went, people sent me home with gifts for Homer, and I was touched by how many remembered to include Scarlett and Vashti as well—hand-crocheted balls stuffed with catnip, little satin-enclosed catnip pillows with each of the cats' names embroidered on them, hand-knitted and hand-sewn kitty blankets, colorful new bowls for food and water, bags of treats, and noisy playthings, like crinkle balls, by the sack.

Of course it was really Homer, and Homer's story, that everybody was interested in. People wanted to hear live accounts of the tales they'd read in the book, to know how Homer was adjusting to his newfound fame. But Homer couldn't travel or deliver speeches himself, so I went as his proxy. I also did interviews with, and wrote articles for, animal-centric magazines and websites, encouraging the adoption of special-needs animals like Homer. As few "famous cats" as there were at the time, there had never (to my knowledge) been a famous special-needs cat, and so Homer became something of a "poster kitty" for the cause of adopting animals once thought unadoptable. I would eventually hear from people who wrote to say that Homer had inspired them to take a chance on a blind—or otherwise disabled—cat. I can honestly say that I've received no fewer than two hundred of these emails over the past few years, and they're always the greatest letters I get.

I traveled to parts of the country I'd never seen in person before—the Deep South, Texas, the Heartland, the Pacific Northwest,

With an FeLV kitty at the
Nine Lives Foundation in
Redwood City, CA

the Rust Belt. I traveled from Minnesota to New Mexico, to Arizona during a heat wave so intense that I could literally feel my *eyeballs* grow warm when I stepped outside. The landscapes would change dramatically each time a plane I was on would land, as would the regional accents, the style of dress, and the local cuisine.

Yet certain things remained constant. I met people of all ages, sizes, religions, and ethnic backgrounds—people who likely would have disagreed vehemently with their counterparts in other regions on everything from politics to place settings (because one would surely consume Alabama hominy grits very differently than Seattle sushi). But the one thing everyone I met agreed about—passionately—was the cause of animal rescue. I can't tell you how many people I've heard, over the last six years, say how much better they think animals are than people. But, personally, I think it's that animals bring out the very best in people—until you can't help but realize how ultimately insignificant the rest of the differences are.

Despite my hectic travel schedule of those few months—

and despite the fact that those crazy days of video and promotional shoots were essentially over—"managing" Homer was still my full-time job. I had to answer his fan mail, oversee his social media presence, regretfully inform those who wrote to say that they would be vacationing in New York—and could they possibly drop by our place to meet Homer in person?—that, unfortunately, Homer wasn't available for personal appearances. "As if Homer were another New York tourist attraction, like the Statue of Liberty," I would say to Laurence.

And *somebody* had to write the thank-you notes for the many gifts Homer received in the mail—as various and plentiful as the gifts I brought home with me from trips. Scarlett and Vashti got their fair share of the bounty, and may, I think, have enjoyed it even more than Homer did. All the soft kitty blankets—that were just her size!—were a profound joy to Scarlett, who'd always loved anything plush and luxurious. To have something soft and warm to claim for her very own, small enough for her to guard from encroachment by the annoying other cats she was forced to live with, was a gift from above. And Vashti loved catnip even more than Homer did. People sent us  catnip they'd grown themselves, on hobby farms or in backyard gardens, and the purity of this home-grown 'nip seemed to make Homer, and especially Vashti, super relaxed and flippy.

For his part, Homer was most enamored of the boxes these gifts came in. He enjoyed them all so much that I couldn't bear to take any away from him—until our living room looked as if we were moving. It was at this point that Laurence tactfully suggested that it might be time to throw at least a few of them away.

As it turned out, there were also quite a few younger readers of *Homer's Odyssey*—elementary and middle-school children who were already passionate about animals, and for whom the message that *different doesn't mean bad* carried more relevance even than it did for adults. One evening, long after the book had been published, a sixth-grade girl came to our apartment with her father, to meet and photograph Homer for an article about him she was writing for *Time For Kids* (*Time* magazine's children's imprint). She took such a grave, shy pleasure in his presence—and Homer was so very gentle with her in his rubbing and head-bonks—that I had to smile at seeing them together. But well before then I'd been hearing from children of about her age who were writing book reports about Homer and wanted me to answer questions they had about the book, or to know what kids like them could do for other special-needs animals. Sometimes they emailed so they could send me pictures of drawings they'd made of Homer, or of Homer-themed arts-and-crafts projects they'd created for school.

It wasn't just in the U.S. and Canada where Homer was gaining a following. Foreign rights to *Homer's Odyssey* had sold in nearly twenty countries before the book was even published, and some of those translations began to appear right around the time the U.S. edition did. I always got a kick out of the foreign editions, the different artwork of their covers, all the various iterations of Homer that differed so greatly from country to country that it was hard to believe they were all publishing the same book. Some countries—like Brazil, France, Russia, and China—used the literal translation of "Homer's Odyssey" as the title for their editions. Others took more of a creative license. In Italy it was *Omero Gatto Nero*, in Germany *Homer und Ich*. In Finland, the book was called *Homer – Kissan Uskomaton Elama,* which meant, *Homer – A Cat's Incredible Life.* The Dutch went with a straightforward *Wonderkat!*, and in Hungary it was simply *Homér*—the book's cover a stark block of solid red, with Homer's name in huge white letters, and in the middle of the cover a very small silhouetted profile of a black cat with a curled tail.

The Japanese title translated roughly into *I See Happy Love.* I'm still unsure as to what the Korean title meant, although I adored

the artwork they included. At the end of the book were several pages of prints depicting vividly hued watercolor paintings, like something from a book of fairy tales. One of them showed a girl who I think was supposed to be me—although she looked like *Alice in Wonderland*—being borne aloft into a starry night by a tuxedoed, flower-bearing, eyeless black cat, trailing a little gray tabby and an even smaller white kitty in the air behind her. A smiling man (Laurence?) waved them all off from a bedroom window.

Homer soon began to receive cards and letters and gifts from the other countries where his story had been published. Somewhere along the line, I realized, he had become not merely *my* cat, but the world's cat.

And yet, he was still just our happy little boy. He had been with me for so long—and while I couldn't say that I took him for granted, he had become as essential, yet also as everyday, as the beating of my own heart.

I would look at Homer sometimes—as he chased a bedeviled Scarlett down the hall, or jumped onto my desk and did his best to keep me from typing, or rolled onto his back to groom the chocolate-and-black fur of his belly—and I would marvel. It was an impossible, an incomprehensible, thing to try to fathom, that so many people all across the globe knew him. Knew him and loved him.

Naturally, Homer had his own Facebook page. It was just a regular personal page at first, but when he reached his 5000-friend limit, I started a "fan" page for him—although I never thought of it that way. Only about a thousand of Homer's Facebook friends followed us to this new page—and even though it grew incrementally, adding perhaps two hundred new followers each month, it still felt like a small, intimate community.

It was Homer's page, and so I wrote there in Homer's voice—not his actual voice, obviously, but the way Homer had always sounded in my own head. I'll admit that I'd never been much for personal photographs, but now we were snapping photos of Homer, Scarlett, and Vashti constantly. I tried to mine our everyday lives for the kinds of things I thought people who'd read the book, and now wanted to keep up with Homer on a day-to-day basis, might find entertaining. *Oh boy! Turkey for dinner!*, I'd write, above a snapshot of Homer doing his best to steal a bit of food from Laurence's plate. Or, **My* little bag of catnip! MINE!* along with a photo of Homer crouched protectively over one of the small bags of home-grown 'nip a friend had sent from her Tennessee farm.

I had a hard time explaining to my mother, when she asked what my workdays now consisted of, that I spent a significant portion of my time pretending to be my cat online.

"But people *do* know that it's really you posting these things, right?" she asked.

"No, mom," I deadpanned. "People think that Homer is climbing onto the keyboard of my computer and typing these things himself."

It was a difficult thing to explain to a parent—although it felt perfectly natural and right to me. People would laugh at "Homer's" daily dispatches, and I was just as apt to laugh and sympathize with the comments and photos they posted themselves. Our regular readers would comment amusingly on my posts detailing Homer's doings, and they would also post pictures and updates about their own cats. I knew more cats on a first-name basis during this time than I ever had before. It might not be strictly accurate to say that I "knew" them—seeing as I'd never actually met them. But, then again, I knew them in the same way our readers knew Homer, through the stories their humans told, the concerns they shared, and the insights they offered when one or another of us would ask questions about preferred litter brands or appropriate diets for aging cats.

This all sounds about as "cat lady" as it gets—so I'll also add that, on occasion, our little community was able to do some real good. Every once in a while a shelter would write to me about an impossible-to-place blind cat and, inevitably, among Homer's community, we would find the perfect home for him. An acquaintance of mine living in Queens discovered two neglected cats in the basement of her apartment building. The building super had put them down there a year earlier, when they were only kittens, for the purpose of keeping the building rat-free. He'd barely thought about them since, and now my friend wanted to find a *real* home for them—one from which they could see the sunlight they'd never once experienced in their lives.

*Homer will never be able to see sunshine, but these two cats can...*my post about them began. Within only a few days, we had half a dozen firm offers of forever homes in the New York area alone. Geoffrey Jennings from Rainy Day Books in Kansas City—a passionate cat lover—offered a trove of autographed, first-edition, collectible books to go along with the cats to their new home. Five days later, all of us in Homer's community were rewarded with a picture of the two cats basking in the sunlight streaming through the bay window of a Brooklyn brownstone. The woman who adopted the cats named them Ellis, after Ellis Island, and Morgan, after the Morgan Library in Manhattan's East Thirties, because the cats had come to her with a library of their own.

We also chipped in small donations, in Homer's community, and were able to raise maybe a thousand dollars or so when natural disasters struck in various parts of the world—the kinds of tragedies that so often affected animals as well as humans, yet during which animals tended to be forgotten. My philosophy was that when you helped animals, you helped people, too—always remembering that the ASPCA, when they'd organized a rescue effort for pets in the wake of 9/11, had also helped people like me in the process. We collected food and other essentials and sent them to where they would do the most good.

Mostly, though, we simply enjoyed each other's company.

Not that everything was all positivity and sunshine. I soon learned that whereas novels are works of fiction, memoirs are true—and while (having written one of each) I'd always been aware of this technical distinction, what I hadn't thought about is that when readers don't like the "character" in your memoir, the person they actually dislike is you, yourself.

I heard from people who thought I was a heartless monster for having thought about my cats on 9/11, a day when so many human lives were lost; I heard from people who thought that I'd married a man who wasn't worthy of Homer; I heard from people who accused me of having adopted Homer twelve years earlier just so I'd someday be able to write a book about him. And I received one very long, very earnest email from an anonymous woman who was convinced that Homer had fallen ill in the months before my wedding because Laurence was slowly poisoning him with a household cleaning agent—in order to get rid of the competition, as it were, for my affections. Calling Laurence a "charismatic and sophisticated alpha male," she warned that he was likely to reveal his true, abusive nature at any moment, and advised me in the strongest possible terms to hire a private investigator to follow him—presumably so as to catch him in the act of being unfaithful.

"Follow me *where?*" Laurence seemed perplexed when I

shared this email with him—albeit tickled at having been described as a *charismatic alpha male*. "You and I both work from home."

"I don't know," I replied. "But I'm going to start marking the levels on the Windex bottle—so don't get any ideas."

Poor Laurence! If only this letter-writer could have seen the grace with which—on the occasions when he joined me on one of my trips—Laurence accepted being referred to as "Mr. Cooper." (His last name is Lerman.)

But these were only a handful of negatives floating in an overwhelmingly positive sea. I had the daily joy of hearing every day from other animal lovers, from rescuers and people who were every bit as crazy about their own cats as I was about mine.

Homer's social-media community would continue to grow over the next couple of years. There was a big jump, after the paperback was published in 2010, when Homer's Facebook following expanded from two thousand to five thousand people within only a few months. But a lot of people seemed to "like" the page and then forget about it—so even when the numbers would appear to indicate otherwise, our core crew stayed more or less the same size.

And, to tell the truth, at the time I liked it that way. Homer didn't have the kind of huge following that seemed likely to sell many books. Then again, I'd never really seen Homer's Facebook page as a place to sell copies of *Homer's Odyssey*. It seemed probable that the only reason someone would follow the page was because they'd read the book already.

And, by then, Homer had gotten to be such a pro at posing for pictures, it seemed a shame to let his talents go to waste.

HOMER'S ONLINE COMMUNITY was always enjoyable, a place where I could post ongoing tales of Homer's amusing antics, a sounding board off of which I could bounce ideas for blog posts or new books as they came to me. But I'll always be truly grateful for the way our internet friends rallied around our family over the next two years, when first Vashti and then Scarlett fell to age-related illnesses.

Ultimately, this is Homer's story. I won't take you too far with me down the paths of confusion and sorrow that Laurence and I traveled during that time—paths well-trodden already by anyone who's loved an animal.

Suffice it to say that between the time when Vashti was diagnosed with chronic renal failure in late 2009, and the time when we lost her in August of 2010, there were many months during which she lived—a life that could only be sustained by a strenuous schedule of home treatment, which seemed overwhelming and impossible for me to undertake when her doctor first explained it. I was positive that I would fail Vashti in ways I couldn't imagine yet.

But, no matter how anxious or bewildered I felt, Homer's community was an unquenchable source of strength and insight.

By far the hardest part of Vashti's new care regimen was administering her every-other-day subcutaneous fluid injections, meant to help her body compensate for her failing kidneys. Vashti was a sweet girl who would tolerate just about anything we did to her, but it was easy to see how much she hated those injections—which weren't simply a shot, but a slow drip that had to be administered over the course of several long minutes. The subQ injections were the only thing Vashti really fought us on (and, bless her heart, she didn't fight hard—she merely struggled). Laurence had to hold her down while I inserted the tiny needle into the back of her neck, and sometimes she squirmed enough that the needle inadvertently hit a tender spot. Her tiny squeaks of pain whenever that happened left me ready to throw in the towel.

Many in Homer's community were old hands at the subQ routine. A few of them suggested a brilliant fix for us—heating the bag containing the solution in a pot of warm water until it came to Vashti's body temperature. This way, Vashti's experience would feel less like being immersed in a cold shower from inside her own body, and more like the pleasant relief of a warm bath.

It was astonishing how immediate the difference was. After our first attempt with this new method, Vashti began to *like* her fluid injections. She would practically bounce with happiness by the time they were over, ready for a recently instituted ritual known as *Vashti's cuddle time.* "It's cuddle time!" Laurence or I would exclaim when the subQ was finished, and we'd climb into bed with Vashti eagerly following. Alone in the bedroom with us—the door closed to keep the other cats out—she would enjoy one uninterrupted hour of exclusive time with both her humans, crawling first onto my chest and purring into my face for a few minutes as I stroked her back, before walking over to Laurence and doing the same with him. She'd spend the whole hour migrating back and forth between

us while the warm fluids we'd just injected spread throughout her body, and when the sixty minutes were up she'd rejoin Scarlett and Homer, cheerful as ever.

It's hard watching an animal you love grow frailer—but Vashti was beautiful right up until the end. She did lose quite a bit of weight, but with her thick, lustrous coat of white fur it was nearly impossible to see, unless you knew her very well. And that fur never lost its silky luster. I have a picture of the two of us taken just days before the end, and in it Vashti literally glows, as if spot-lit from an unseen source.

The eternal feminine was what Laurence said of Vashti on her last day. It was something Lee Strasberg had said about Marilyn Monroe at her funeral, a way of describing the timeless, imperishable quality of her beauty—a beauty so overpowering, yet also so vulnerable, that it could reach right out and squeeze your heart until it ached.

Camille on her deathbed had nothing on our Vashti.

The paperback edition of *Homer's Odyssey* came out less than a month after we lost her. This time around, my publisher did spring for a small book tour—and, even though it wasn't near any of the four cities they'd originally planned to send me to, I insisted that the first stop be at Blind Cat Rescue & Sanctuary in North Carolina.

I'd seen pictures of many other blind cats since Homer's story was first published, but I still hadn't met many in the flesh. It was a moving experience to walk through Blind Cat Rescue, to enter room after room full of cats—cats who were young and old; white, gray, tabby, and calico; cats who were large and cats who were small; some who had long silky fur like Vashti's, and some who had practically no fur at all—but who all, nevertheless, looked like Homer. They raised questioning noses into the air just like Homer did, turned their heads from side to side like sonar dishes as they tried to "see" with their ears. And, even without eyes, their faces still managed to convey the joy they'd found in their life with each other, and with their human caregivers.

Vashti may only have been a supporting player in *Homer's Odyssey*. But in our lives—our *real* lives—she'd always had one of three starring roles. Reading from Homer's book now, choosing a passage that included Vashti and Scarlett as well as Homer, and having just seen so many other "unadoptable" cats like Homer who'd nevertheless found happiness in loving arms, was the first time I felt truly whole since Vashti had left us.

THERE WAS DECIDEDLY less *Homer* on Homer's Facebook page while all this was going on, but those core few who'd been with us from the beginning never complained or abandoned us. And they remained with us still in February of 2011, when Scarlett developed a sarcoma high on her left hind leg, the result of the rabies vaccination she'd gotten years earlier in Miami. (The specific formula that caused this sarcoma in some cats has been discontinued, by the way; you should always vaccinate your cats against rabies.)

In some ways, it was harder with Scarlett as her illness progressed than it had been with Vashti—not because it was so much worse or made her suffer more. But Scarlett had always been such a surly, feisty, irascible girl. She'd been born irritated with everybody and everything—even in her youth, she'd been the mean old lady who yells, *Get off my lawn, you kids!* Our other cats bothered her.

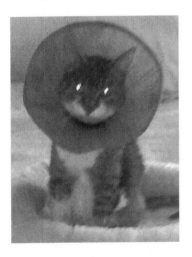

Laurence's mere existence—his insistence on living with us, despite her having made it perfectly clear that she'd prefer he left—was an ongoing annoyance. Guests in our home had obviously been sent by the devil himself, just so they could coo at her and make other friendly, insulting gestures until she was forced—in a state of high dudgeon—to *harrumph* her way into the seclusion of a bedroom. There were only two things in the world that Scarlett truly enjoyed—one of them was food, and the other was me. Anybody else, human or feline, was quickly reminded with a sharp *rowr!* and disciplinary smack of her paw to maintain their distance, leaving her to enjoy her wide berth of personal space in dignified peace.

Scarlett mellowed a great deal, however, during those last months—and I'll admit that it made me sad to see her become more accepting and tolerant as her health failed. I do think, though, that this change was partly because Homer was so considerate of her. He slept nearer to her than he'd ever dared before. But he no longer chased her, no longer tried to insert himself into her games of "chase the paper ball," no longer bothered her in any way. He stayed closer to Scarlett than he had in earlier years, but his closeness was far less intrusive.

We'd hoped that surgery to remove her tumor would solve the problem—and, when it didn't, we had difficult decisions to make. There were many in Homer's community who advocated for removing Scarlett's leg altogether. But Scarlett was nearly seventeen, and arthritic, and she'd always been so poised and self-possessed that forcing her, at this point in her life, to adjust to getting around on only three legs seemed almost cruel. The same was true of chemotherapy. Others among our online friends had made different decisions for their own cats under similar circumstances. But everybody understood that Scarlett was Scarlett, and that there was no one-size-fits-all solution to these kinds of problems.

Scarlett had become so quiet and tractable by the time we knew it was over, in December of 2011, that it was almost as if she wasn't there anymore. She was the first cat I'd ever lived with, and there was a special pain in her loss. When I brought her to the vet for the last time, I couldn't even give my name to the receptionist without bursting into tears.

But Scarlett had one last gift for me. She'd been so silent and immobile in her carrier that I wasn't even sure she was still awake. But when the doctor very gently inserted the needle into her neck, Scarlett's eyes—which had been glazed and unfocused for the past day—quickly sharpened and narrowed. I knew by now that a needle so small, injected into the relatively insensitive scruff of her neck, wouldn't hurt her. But Scarlett still had enough of her personal dignity left to resent that a stranger had dared touch her at all. With her typical churlish *rowr!* of old, she reached up out of her cloth, blanket-lined carrier to take an annoyed swipe at the vet's hand. *Get off my lawn, you kids!*

It was so quintessentially *Scarlett* that I couldn't help but chuckle through my tears. *There's my surly girl!* For that brief moment, she wasn't the ailing, compliant Scarlett of the last few months. She was once again the crusty curmudgeon I'd loved so well for so long.

I would always say after that, in describing her final moments, that Scarlett had gotten to die as she'd lived—really, *really* pissed off.

HOMER TRULY GRIEVED when we lost Scarlett, and Homer's community grieved with us. After about three days, when it became clear that she wasn't coming back, Homer seemed to age overnight. His customary run slowed to a walk, and his walk took on the stiff, wide-legged gait of an old man. He was no longer interested in chasing crumpled balls of paper across the living room, or in demanding bits of turkey from Laurence's sandwiches. Even a fresh sprinkling of home-grown catnip on the rug would leave him apathetic.

It was heartbreaking to see the transformation—made painfully ironic by the certainty I felt that Scarlett herself would have been perfectly content to be the last cat standing. As far as Scarlett was concerned, the best days of her life had been the earliest ones, when she was an only cat.

But Homer had always thought about his relationship with Scarlett very differently than Scarlett did. In Homer's mind, Scarlett was the (unwitting) supporting player in a thousand stalk-and-pounce adventure tales Homer liked to tell himself. She was his foil, his muse, his great nemesis, and he was never happier than when he'd finally succeeded in irritating her to the point that she would swat at him, nip at his neck, and then chase him down the hall before turning around to let him chase her back into the bedroom. While she hadn't been especially playful during her last months, she'd still been *there*—a comforting presence and warm scent, familiar for as long as he could remember, against which Homer could curl up and doze contentedly.

But it wasn't just the loss of Scarlett herself. Equally hard on Homer, I think, was the fact that he was now alone whenever

Laurence and I were out. We had the luxury of spending far more time with Homer than most cat parents could with their own, simply because we worked from our apartment—but, still, we couldn't be home *all* the time. A trip to the vet, while unpleasant for all concerned (Homer's deep-seated hatred of the vet's office having only grown more intense with time), revealed that—physically, at least—he was in fine health.

What Homer needed more than anything was a new friend.

I thought that an older, more seasoned adult cat might make an ideal companion for Homer. Accordingly, I pulled first one owner-surrendered cat—and, when she and Homer didn't "click," another—from the euthanization lists at a New York open-intake shelter. My plan was to foster these cats and, if things worked out, to let them become "foster failures"—permanent members of our family.

There's always a period of adjustment when two adult cats get to know each other. Even in understanding this, however, things seemed particularly rough between Homer and first one, then the other, of the new cats we tried introducing him to. Poor Homer was utterly incapable of picking up on the visual body language of a wary cat. He had no way of seeing the arched back, the puffed tail, the backward steps of a cat who was unsure if Homer's approach was friendly or hostile. Scarlett and Vashti had known him since he was a kitten, and had grown accustomed to his seemingly odd ways. But to the cats we brought home now, Homer's eyeless black face must have appeared completely expressionless. He would approach them for a friendly, *how ya doin'?* mutual sniff, and was met with nothing but aggressive rebuffs.

Truth be told, I probably could have made it work with at least one of the cats if I'd really put the time in. But I didn't have the heart to subject Homer to any more stress after the loss of his two best friends. So I worked with a couple of the no-kill shelters I'd developed relationships with, and eventually we were able to find forever homes for both our fosters. (I still get pictures of them from their happy adoptive humans, and it always makes me smile.)

And that was how, early in 2012, we ended up adopting two little black kittens—litter-mates named Clayton and Fanny. Clayton had a damaged hind leg that we knew from the beginning would most likely have to come off sooner or later. (As it turned out—sooner.)

I'll tell their story in full later on. For now, it's enough to know that, even by kitten standards, Clayton and Fanny were ridiculously cheerful and high-spirited. There's probably nothing more irresistible than a kitten who adores you—and our kittens adored their new big brother immediately, right from the start. They were so playful, so eager to please, so ready to worship Homer in an abject, shameless way, that Homer would have had to be much more hard-hearted than he was to resist their charms. Homer couldn't see the goofy way Clayton would excitedly bunny-hop beside him on his three good legs, but I think Homer could sense it—and before long he was running, leaping, and chasing after toys, over the furniture and off the walls of our home, with all his old zest.

Ultimately, Homer recovered because he wasn't made for grief. It wasn't just that he was too innately happy—he was also too strong. Homer's strength was a force of nature, his will to live indomitable, as we would soon come to learn. All he needed in order to heal was a reminder that the world was still full of joy—that joy itself had been, and always would be, the very substance of his life.

I, of course, had known this about Homer all along. I'd written an entire book about it.

Playing the role of big brother was a new adventure for Homer. And new adventures were what Homer had always lived for.

Strong Like Bull

**There is a time for many words, and
there is also a time for sleep.**

-HOMER, *The Odyssey*

IT WAS A COLD, GRAY AFTERNOON IN EARLY DECEMBER, AND I was pulling our freshly cleaned winter bedding from the laundry basket, planning to swap it for the lighter sheets and blanket currently dressing our bed. Homer and the kittens (who had, by now, grown into full-fledged cats) were sitting in a semi-circle on the floor at the foot of the bed. "Helping" me change the linens was always a popular activity among our three. Homer would perform the vital job of attacking each corner of the bed as the fitted sheet went over it. Fanny pitched in by diving under the top sheet and creating a lump I couldn't work around until I'd pushed her onto the floor. And Clayton, not as good a jumper as the other two, would dig in his front claws and haul himself up onto the bed—dragging blanket and sheets halfway to the floor—and hop around after the other two until I said, in an exasperated voice, "That's *enough!*" at which point he would flop down and look at me with deep reproach for having spoiled the game.

It was unquestionably a frustrating way to make the bed, but I couldn't help but smile now as I saw Homer's face turned up to mine in anticipation of one of our oldest and most cherished rituals. Homer was fifteen years old, and more apt than he'd used to be to choose naps over play. Where once he'd been the "poster kitty" for special-needs animals, he was now more of an elder statesman. His one gray whisker had become six, and the ebony sheen of his head was flecked with gray as well. Fanny and Clayton had helped him recover the *joie de vivre* he'd lost after Scarlett's passing a year earlier. Still, I was bringing out the heavier blankets sooner than I normally would—usually I'd wait for the first snow—because I thought Homer might appreciate the additional warmth and softness a bit earlier this year.

I'd just gotten the old sheets off and dumped the new fitted sheet onto the middle of the bed, when I noticed that Homer, resting on his haunches, wobbled a bit before falling over to one side. He quickly righted himself, but fell over to the side again. Then he tried to stand, but his legs wouldn't support him. He went down in a small heap and curled all four paws beneath his body.

At first I wasn't even sure that I'd seen what I thought I saw. Maybe Homer was just lying down, and I had only imagined that something seemed "off." But then I saw how Homer struggled to hold his head up, like a kitten fighting to stay awake while falling asleep on his feet, and I knew that something was very wrong.

"Laurence!" In two long strides I was in the hallway and buried halfway to my chest in the hall closet as I struggled to free one of the cat carriers from its storage place. Clayton and Fanny had followed eagerly (*She opened the closet! Closets are awesome!*) and I shooed them away impatiently. "*Laurence!*" I called again, and found that Laurence had already abandoned his home office next to our bedroom and was standing beside me.

"What happened?" he asked.

"There's something wrong with Homer. He just…fell over." I spoke calmly, not wanting to alarm Homer, who was always so attuned to the sound of my voice. "We have to get him to the animal hospital."

Laurence regarded me for a fraction of a second. It was only when I saw his face tighten with concern that I knew what my own looked like, despite the forced evenness of my tone. "Let's go," was all he said, and went to round up keys, coats, and cell phones.

Getting Homer into his carrier was usually an onerous task. Once upon a time, a trip in the carrier had meant a move to a new home and new territories for Homer to explore. But we'd lived here with Laurence for just over seven years now—nearly half of Homer's life. These days, the carrier meant only one thing: the vet. There was nothing in the world Homer loathed and feared as much as the vet's office. He'd never exactly been a *good* patient, but the problem had gotten exponentially worse over the years. The last time we'd gone, in January, I'd had to cradle Homer in my arms in order for the vet to get close enough to draw a blood sample. When the needle went in, Homer had panicked and bitten my hand so hard that I'd had to go the emergency room later for a tetanus shot. He'd seemed immediately remorseful upon hearing my yelp of pain, struggling to get his front paws onto my shoulder so he could nuzzle my neck, the way he had that very first day we'd met, all those years ago. When the vet had tried to approach him again, he'd hissed at her wildly over my shoulder, like a thing possessed. *Leave me alone!* he seemed to say. *Look what you made me do to my human!*

We hadn't been back since.

Homer didn't struggle at all now. He was still breathing, and he appeared to be awake. But whether he was on the floor or in his carrier seemed to be a matter of equal indifference to him.

Seeing his utter lack of resistance made the knots in my stomach tighten. I held him for a moment, pressing my cheek to the top of his head before gently lowering him in. "You're going to be fine," I assured him in a soft voice. "You'll be just fine."

It was the lunch hour—always a difficult time to catch a cab in front of our Midtown apartment—so Laurence walked a couple of blocks up while I huddled Homer in his carrier as close under my coat as I could, trying to keep him warm. With my cell phone cradled between my shoulder and my ear, I let the receptionist at the vet's office know that Homer and I were on our way in with an emergency. As I hung up, I saw the blessed sight of Laurence in the back of a cab pulling up to us.

Homer didn't budge or call out once during the entire ten-minute ride—also very unlike him—and I found myself unable to stop unzipping the top of the carrier just far enough to slip my hand in, to stroke Homer's head and side and make sure he was still breathing. The traffic on First Avenue was too heavy for our cabbie to cross, forcing him to drop us across the street from the animal hospital's entrance. I left Laurence to pay him and, like the true New Yorker I'd long-since become, darted into the street against the light, breaking into a run so none of the oncoming cars would have to slow to avoid me. I was slightly out of breath by the time I reached the receptionist's desk and placed Homer in his carrier on top of it.

Reina, the woman behind the desk, knew me well. I'd been there at least once a month during the two years when Vashti and Scarlett were sick, and more recently when Clayton had to have his hind leg removed. Laurence and I liked to say that we'd probably financed a Cooper-Lerman Memorial Wing of the animal hospital, given our outrageous expenses there over the past few years. It was a joke, of course, but I don't think I'd ever felt less like laughing than I did in that moment, finding myself yet again in that familiar waiting room.

"What happened?" Reina asked, making sympathetic clucking sounds at Homer through the mesh sides of the carrier.

"I don't know. He just kind of fell over," I told her.

Reina pressed a button on her phone that summoned a vet tech through the swinging door that led to the exam rooms in the back. She took the carrier from Reina but turned to stop me when I tried to follow. "You'll have to wait out here," she said kindly, but firmly.

"But I have to go with him." My voice was calm. *Just two reasonable people having a reasonable disagreement.* "He's blind, and he's terrified of the vet's office. I don't think you'll be able to handle him without me."

She peered at Homer, silent and stone-still in his carrier. He'd always been a little guy, but now he looked positively frail. "I think we'll manage." She smiled reassuringly. "We have to bring him to the tech area for tests," she explained, "and there are other animals back there. That's why we need you to wait out here."

I turned to Reina, who was also our pet-sitter when we traveled and knew Homer better than anyone else at the clinic, hoping for a reprieve. "He'll be fine, *mami.*" Behind her, the vet tech had already disappeared with Homer back through the swinging door. "He's so out of it, he probably won't even know what's going on."

I TOOK THE seat Laurence had saved for me in the cozy, wood-paneled waiting area—made welcoming with posters of puppies and kittens, flyers for pet-sitters, and copies of *Best Friends* magazine—and tried to imagine what went on when a nearly unconscious cat was brought into a veterinary emergency room. My sole knowledge of what happened when someone was rushed unconscious to the hospital came from television and movies. Would they plop Homer onto a gurney and wheel him speedily into another room while a doctor called for CCs of this and tests for that? Would nurses cluster around trying to get blood pressure and pulse readings? I was heartsick, miserable at the thought of Homer—tiny Homer, weakened and terrified—being subjected to unknown probes and prods and lord-only-knew-what-else without me there to comfort him.

But, as it turned out, I was luckier than I realized. I wouldn't have to wonder for long.

The tech area, where Homer had been taken, was all the way in the back of the building, and the waiting area was in the front. Separating them was a long corridor with exam rooms branching off from it. We were probably a good hundred feet away from Homer, with two closed doors (one at either end of the corridor) between us. Nevertheless, within a few minutes I heard what was going on.

Everybody heard what was going on.

Over the years, I've probably heard the full range of sounds that the average housecat is capable of making—the meows, burbles, and coos; the purring and deep-throated whines; the shrill, unforgettable screams of a cat who's enraged or terrified. Homer himself had always had an especially rich vocal repertoire, with a series of highly distinct mews, yips, and growls meant to indicate things like, *I can't find you; I'm hungry; I'm coming over to be petted now;* and *This is irritating me.*

What I heard now wasn't any of those. It hardly even sounded like noises a cat should be capable of making—and, at first, I didn't think it *was* a cat. I didn't even think that the sound came from any natural source. For a second, I thought that maybe a nearby construction worker had started up a chainsaw. But, after the briefest of pauses for breath, it became clear that these were animal noises—the sound of some enraged wild beast fending off hunters or defending its territory. The vicious, furious snarls rose in volume to fill the entire waiting room, so deep now, so sustained, so impossibly loud, that they could only be described as roars.

It was lunchtime, the busiest time of day at the animal clinic, and the waiting room was packed. There were huge dogs and tiny ones at the ends of leashes, cats and rabbits in carriers, two cages containing a parrot and a parakeet. Every animal was accompanied by a human, and it was something of a miracle that Laurence had managed to score us two seats at all.

As the roars from the back of the hospital continued and grew in both volume and anger, the comfortable hum of conversation and scuffling animals in the waiting room fell silent. Reina, from her station behind the receptionist's desk, put the call she was taking on hold and turned to stare in open-mouthed wonder at the door leading to the back. For a breathless moment, the entire animal hospital was dead silent except for the enraged clamor rising from the back. Then a hushed murmuring rose in the waiting room, as if everybody was instinctively wary of elevating their voices above a whisper. *What the...? What's going on back there? What* is *that?* One woman, in an undertone, said something that ended with...*a panther?* The man she was with muttered darkly about the kind of idiot who thought it was okay to keep exotic pets in a New York apartment.

Two large dogs had begun to whimper and cringed behind the legs of their owners, while a smaller dog issued a low rumble, the hackles raised on the back of his neck. From the dark recesses of carriers, I heard hisses and growls. The parakeet twittered and fluttered frantically around his cage. I thought of my younger sister, who'd always shrieked so loudly and continuously when receiving childhood shots that every other kid in the pediatrician's waiting room would break into terrified sobs.

"What do you think it is?" Laurence whispered to me.

I threw him a wry, sideways look.

"You think that's *Homer?*" Laurence appeared dubious. But then his glance took in my face, which felt so hot that I knew it had to be fiery red. His expression changed from incredulity to awe. "Damn," he muttered.

I was already standing when the door to the back swung open, and I nearly walked right into the vet tech who'd initially brought Homer to the back of the hospital. She'd been so calm and confident when we'd first come in, but now she was profoundly flustered. Her face looked as red as mine had felt a moment ago, and I could see that her hands were trembling. "They need you back there," she blurted. Pointing down the hallway, she added, "The last exam room on the left." Once she'd made sure I was going the right way, she ducked into a small side room, quickly closing the door behind her.

I felt a bit like a character in a scary movie as I headed in the direction the vet tech had indicated—some not-very-bright girl inexplicably walking toward the room containing the terrifying monster, rather than away from it. I'd known that the sounds I'd heard in the waiting room would only grow louder as I approached their source, but it was still unnerving to hear *how much* louder they became.

The tableau that greeted me when I reached Homer's exam room might have been comical under different circumstances. Standing in a semicircle—facing the high metal exam table bolted to the wall, but at a judicious distance from it—were three women. One was the doctor, who must have been new to the practice, because I'd never seen her before. The other two were clearly assistants. They'd donned long, thickly padded gloves that stretched from the tips of their fingers all the way up to their shoulders, like the ones that falconers wear. They'd also knotted bandanas behind their ears and pulled them up protectively over their faces. Their foreheads above the bandanas were a vivid pink and beaded with sweat. Their bodies were poised with a tense wariness, leaning slightly forward at the shoulders while their feet were half-turned in the opposite direction, ready to carry them back to a safer distance if the need arose.

Seeing Homer—all four pounds of him, crouched

defensively on the exam table—took me back instantly, all the way to that summer night more than twelve years earlier, when a Homer I hadn't recognized had chased a large male intruder right out of our Miami apartment. If he'd looked helpless and fragile a half-hour ago, when I'd first brought him in to the clinic, he now more closely resembled the panther the woman in the waiting room had thought she'd heard. The hind part of his body was elevated and his chest was lowered until it almost touched the table beneath him. His head was raised with his mouth wide open, lips pulled back in a cruel rictus that bared all his teeth. His head and ears moved evenly from side to side as he listened for a cue as to where the next assault might come from, one paw raised with claws at full extension, ready to lash out as soon as someone came within striking distance.

One of the assistants was holding a yellowish hand towel in front of her, the way a lion tamer might hold a chair between himself and the roaring lion before him. As I entered, the assistant—still maintaining a safe distance between herself and Homer—gingerly tossed it over his head. Homer immediately erupted into a fresh round of anguished, deafening roars, thrashing angrily as his claws attempted to escape the towel and find his tormentors.

I knew that putting a towel over the head of a distressed cat was standard procedure, that it usually *calmed* them, and that the hot bolt of rage that stabbed from my chest to my belly was therefore unwarranted. Everybody in that room wanted only to help Homer. Still, it took a wrenching effort of will to make my voice sound as serene as it needed to, for Homer's sake.

"Okay, so Homer is blind." I said *Homer* in the gentle, sing-song cadence I used at home when I was particularly happy with him. The wild thrashing beneath the towel stilled. "Putting a cloth over his head isn't going to quiet him the way it does other cats. You're just making him more upset."

The assistant who'd thrown the towel now leaned forward and, grabbing the corner closest to her and farthest from Homer's claws, quickly pulled it off while simultaneously taking a large step back. The Homer thus revealed, puffed up to several times his normal size, bore little resemblance to the Homer I knew. Nevertheless, his ears had pricked up and turned toward my voice. Once freed from the towel, his nose followed, rising inquisitively in an attempt to discern whether there was a familiar scent to match the familiar cadence.

"You're a good boy, Homer." I approached him slowly, my hands raised in front of me in an instinctive gesture of non-threatening compliance that was, of course, wasted on a blind cat. Cautiously, I put one hand directly beneath his nose.

Homer immediately pressed his whole face into my cupped palm, and I used the other hand to rub gently behind his ears. As frightening as it had been to see Homer in his rage, my heart nearly broke now to see him morph back into his normal self—just a scared little cat, terrified out of his wits at being separated from the human he trusted. "You're a good boy, Homer, a good, good boy," I repeated soothingly, and Homer's fur sank as his entire body seemed to relax.

If I'd levitated into the air right in front of them, the vet and her assistants couldn't have appeared more gobsmacked as Homer transformed from snarling beast to docile housecat in my hands. "I'm sorry," the vet said. "With the way he was brought in, we didn't know he'd put up such a fight."

I told you so! I told you so! a voice in my brain shrieked. But I only laughed ruefully and said, "I understand. It *is* hard to believe that such a little guy can make such a big ruckus."

"He's so *teeny!*" one of the assistants exclaimed almost indignantly, as if she'd been trying to restrain herself but couldn't hold it in any longer—couldn't quite fathom how one small cat, and a sick one at that, had been able to cause three grown women who handled animals *for a living* to fear legitimately for their physical safety.

"Maybe you should spend a few minutes alone with him,"

the vet said now. "It looks like we'll have to sedate him before we can examine him. That might go easier if he's a little calmer before I try to inject him."

"That's a good idea," I said. "Is it okay if I sit on the floor?"

At her nod, I sat down cross-legged about a foot from the exam table. "Come here, Homer-Bear," I said, and Homer leapt a touch awkwardly from the table to the ground. In the crouched, creeping way of an animal that suspects it's being hunted, he made his way over to where I sat and crawled into my lap. The three women, still shaking their heads in amazement, filed silently out of the room.

Homer and I sat there for long minutes as I continued to stroke him. He didn't purr, and he didn't fall asleep, but he did fall into a calm, quiet reverie. *My poor boy,* I thought. *My poor, poor boy.* At this point, I felt well beyond guilty and heartily sorry that I'd brought Homer in at all, knowing how very traumatic the vet always was for him—although what choice had I had? Eventually, the vet returned and knelt over us just long enough to jab a needle into the back of Homer's neck. Homer instantly hissed and reared up, trying to catch her with his front claws. But the sedative kicked in pretty quickly, and Homer fell unconscious back into my lap.

"We can take it from here," the vet said, lifting Homer and bundling him back into his carrier. "We'll draw blood and run some tests. I'll let you know when he's ready to leave."

Laurence and I had to wait another half hour before we were able to bring a still-sedated Homer back home. I was given some instructions on how to care for him and things to watch for until the sedative wore off. "Do you know what caused him to fall over like that this afternoon?" I asked. After all the drama of the preceding hour, the thing that had brought us there in the first place seemed almost like an afterthought, like something that had happened years ago to somebody else.

"We'll know more when the bloodwork comes back

tomorrow," the vet told me. "We'll call you as soon as we have it. The important thing now is for him to get some rest."

HOMER SLEPT FOR the rest of the afternoon. He didn't stir into consciousness again until early evening, when he woke just long enough to eat his dinner before staggering back into the bedroom and collapsing in the little nest I'd made for him on the floor from old t-shirts and sweaters. I moved his litter-box into our bedroom and kept him in there with us overnight, away from the curious noses of Clayton and Fanny, who couldn't figure out why their big brother smelled so different (like the vet's office, although they didn't know it),  and why he didn't wake and acknowledge them, even when they touched his head and face with tentative little paws. At some point in the middle of the night, Homer made an unsuccessful attempt to jump onto the bed but fell over backwards, the sedative having still not worn off entirely. I didn't want him on the bed—which, being a king-size, was rather high off the ground—because I wasn't sure he'd be able to jump off without hurting himself if he needed his litter-box. But I also didn't want him to have to sleep by himself. I ended up moving my pillows and a blanket down to the floor, so I could curl up next to him.

The next morning, Homer was almost miraculously back to his old self. He ate a big breakfast and greeted Clayton and Fanny in his usual imperious way. A couple of hours later we were playing one of his favorite games, wherein I would wriggle my finger under the bed covers and Homer (who could once again get on and off the bed just fine) would pounce on them. I was delighted to see him cocking his head to one side in familiar fashion as he listened for the slight noises that would pinpoint where, exactly, my fingers were.

He was still doing well enough when noon came around that Laurence and I went out to grab a quick lunch at a sandwich place next to our apartment building. We'd just placed our orders when my cell phone rang with a call from the animal hospital. The vet who called wasn't the one who had seen Homer yesterday, but she assured me that she'd thoroughly read both Homer's test results and his medical file.

"How's he doing today?" she asked.

"He seems okay, actually." I'd risen and was walking through the restaurant, so we could continue the call outside where I wouldn't disturb the diners around me. "He was even playing this morning."

She sounded surprised. "He was *playing*?"

I think I mistook her surprise for reproach—as if she were implying that I was a dangerous lunatic for running an invalid cat like Homer around—and I quickly backtracked. "It wasn't *strenuous* play. He was in a playful mood, is what I meant."

"No, that's good!" She seemed to file this tidbit away for future reference before continuing. "So I've looked over the bloodwork and Homer's file, and I wanted to go over the results with you."

She started with the numbers that fell within the normal range and therefore looked good, and that was the shortest part of our conversation. The problem, it quickly became clear, was Homer's liver. I didn't have to understand all the ins and outs or medical jargon to know immediately how serious the problem was. Doing some rapid calculations, I realized that Homer's liver values (the enzymes that were supposed to be found in the liver itself, not in his bloodstream) were about fifteen hundred percent higher than what was normal in a cat. *Fifteen hundred percent!* "If his fur wasn't so black, you'd probably have noticed a while ago that his ears are yellow, and how jaundiced he is," the vet told me, and I cursed myself for having been so stupid—so unforgivably stupid and unobservant. "I sounded surprised when you said Homer was playing this morning, because frankly a cat with numbers like these shouldn't even be able to walk." She didn't say it aloud, but I knew what she was thinking: *He shouldn't even be alive.*

My mind instantly rejected that thought. Numbers or no numbers, anybody with two eyes in their head could see that Homer was still *Homer*. He ate, he played, he cuddled in my lap. Maybe on paper he shouldn't be alive, but in the real world he was still walking around the same as ever—and where there was life, there was hope. So I took a deep breath to steady myself and asked, "Where do we go from here?"

"I'd like you to bring Homer in this afternoon," the vet said, "and plan on leaving him here for a few days—maybe a week." She launched into her recommended course of treatment, an aggressive one that would involve hooking Homer up round-the-clock to various drips and medications, which would drain harmful fluids out and introduce healthier ones in, and give his liver a fighting chance to recover.

I didn't even know I'd started to cry until I became aware of a pain on my cheeks, and realized that the icy December wind had frozen the tears to my face. *My god,* was all I could think. *My god, how can I do this to him? How can I bring him back to that place and leave him there all alone?*

"Let me talk to the doctor who saw Homer yesterday," the vet concluded. "I'll call you back so we can make a plan."

Laurence was waiting at our table when I re-entered the restaurant, and I saw that our food had arrived in my absence. I couldn't touch mine, however, and as I relayed to Laurence the substance of my conversation with the vet, my tears began to flow in earnest. He reached across the table to cover my hand with his and tried to say something comforting. I suddenly became aware that we were in a very public place, and that the other patrons closest to us were beginning to take an interest in our table. "I'm sorry," I said, and my voice sounded like I was choking. "I have to go back outside. People will think you're breaking up with me." I got up and left him for a second time, crouching once I'd reached the sidewalk again and putting my head between my legs as I tried to pull myself together.

I was still outside, grateful for the cold air I inhaled in greedy gulps in the hopes it would clear my thoughts, when the vet called back. "I spoke with the doctor who saw Homer yesterday," she told me. "We talked a bit and…" She hesitated, as if searching for the right words. "We're not sure that Homer would benefit from a hospital environment."

For a moment, I was hopeful. "You mean you think I can treat him at home?"

Her voice softened. "Look, the doctor you saw yesterday told me what happened. We can't get near Homer without sedating him, and we can't keep a cat fully sedated for days at a time. And we can't sedate a cat at *all* with bloodwork like Homer's. If we'd known how bad his numbers were, we wouldn't have sedated him yesterday."

"So you're saying you can't treat him without sedating him, but you can't sedate him until you've been able to treat him."

"That's about it," the vet agreed. "The thing is, even the really mean cats, when they have numbers like these, are usually so sick and weak that we can do whatever we need to with them. I don't know how much longer Homer's strength can last—it's a miracle that it's lasted this long—but as long as it does, there's really nothing to be gained by you bringing him back here."

She was, as I would later recount at innumerable shelter readings whenever I told this story, saying to me in the nicest possible way, *Please don't ever bring your demon cat back to our animal hospital again.* I couldn't argue. I was no more anxious to bring Homer back than they were to have him.

"Is there anything I can do for him by myself?"

"I'm going to write you a couple of prescriptions," she said. "Some medication to support his liver and other functions. There's a pharmacy uptown that can compound it with something yummy-tasting like chicken or tuna. That way you can just squirt it into his mouth or mix it with his food, instead of trying to pill him. It's a two-week course of treatment."

My voice cracked when I spoke again, dreading the answer even before I asked the question. "What do we do for him when the two weeks are up?"

"I'm sorry," she said, and the sorrow in her voice was genuine. "But Homer's numbers are incompatible with life."

It was an awful phrase, *incompatible with life*—at once so brutal yet efficiently descriptive that it told the whole story. So it seemed almost superfluous when she went on to add:

"I don't think he has more than two weeks left."

As a kindness to my fellow sensitive readers (and I'm assuming that applies to most of you reading this), I'll risk ruining the suspense and tell you up front that we did *not* lose Homer within the next two weeks. Nor did we lose him within four weeks, or even four months. Homer, as it turned out, had more fight left in him than even those of us who knew him best (and had seen him at his worst) thought he was capable of. In the end, he would stay with us for the better part of the next year.

But, at the time, we still had to go through it all and make our decisions without knowing outcomes. Looking back now, I realize that I didn't really have any decisions to make. Homer had made them already. All I could do was let things take whatever course they were going to take. But I didn't know this then—or perhaps it's more honest to say that it was a knowledge I resisted.

It was hard to believe that Homer's condition could really be as dire as the vet had said. I scanned his ears anxiously when

Laurence and I got home from the restaurant, and indeed, when I looked at them closely, the insides had a definite yellow cast beneath the black of his fur. But Homer quickly grew impatient with his ear exam. He was far more interested in the bag I'd brought home containing my uneaten sandwich. After downing a generous helping of sliced turkey—which pretty much depleted my sandwich entirely, and it was astonishing to watch Homer put away a quantity of food that would have more than filled *me* up—Homer trotted over to his bed on the desk beside my computer, waiting patiently for me to sit down after lunch as I usually did, and spend the afternoon typing away with him by my side. It was as if yesterday hadn't happened.

I spent the next two weeks on a sort of doomsday watch. Every time Homer ate a meal with gusto (which was pretty much every meal), I counted it as a triumph. Every time I watched him chase a crinkle ball around, every time he cuddled up to have me spoon him on the couch, I thought, *Is this it? Is this the last time?* Every time he was slower to awaken from a nap than I thought he should be, I wondered if he was going to wake up at all.

I watched and I wondered—and I agonized. What was I to do for him? When Vashti had been diagnosed with chronic renal failure (and hyperthyroidism, and high blood pressure, and anemia), I'd forced pills down her throat once a day, and given her shots twice a day, and administered subcutaneous fluid injections every other day. I'd taken her to the vet for monthly check-ups and twice she'd had to stay there overnight. Scarlett had had surgery for her cancer, and I'd had to give her insulin shots twice a day for her diabetes. Certainly none of it could be described as *fun*—and the two of them had struggled and fled and clawed and even hissed on occasion enough for me to know how much they disliked all the poking and prodding and pilling—but all that had been a few unpleasant minutes out of our days, which the two of them seemed to forget completely as soon as it was over. And the reward for those unpleasant few minutes was the additional time we had together that we wouldn't have had otherwise.

But Homer wasn't like Vashti and Scarlett. For the past few years, he wouldn't even let me trim his claws anymore. I had known even before Homer got sick—back when I was going through everything I went through with my two girls—that I wouldn't be able to do the same for him. Regular vet visits would be difficult enough, probably even impossible. As much as Homer loved and trusted me, I knew he'd never let me pill him regularly, or stick needles in him. The best-case scenario was that I'd win those battles (maybe!) but end up injured and bloodied for my efforts, and Homer would come to fear my scent and the sound of my voice as much as he'd ever feared the vet's office. Homer would never understand why I was doing all these terrible things to him. What would be the point of extending his life only to rob him of all the security and love and trust he'd built that life on?

There would be no point, I had assured myself, back when Homer was healthy and these were only abstract thoughts.

But now the abstract had become concrete, and the sand beneath my feet had shifted. I couldn't just do nothing, could I? I mean, maybe I couldn't do *anything*—but I certainly couldn't do *nothing*. The collective wisdom of Homer's Facebook community recommended milk thistle, which I began liberally sprinkling into his drinking water. Perhaps it helped. But it certainly didn't seem like the kind of heroic measures I should be taking on his behalf. How could a few drops of milk thistle be sufficient when I was willing to do anything—literally, *anything*—that could be done for Homer, if only he would let me help him?

I remember one day when it was especially bad with me, when the certainty that I was losing Homer and could do nothing to stop it was the only certainty I had in the world, and it sat in my chest so heavily I could hardly breathe. I was at my computer, and Homer was sitting on his haunches on the desk next to me, leaning the entire weight of his body heavily against my left shoulder, as he did when he sensed that I needed comfort. I went to his Facebook page and, unlike my usual habit of posting funny pictures and amusing little stories, typed a single sentence. *How will I live without this cat?* I quickly deleted it, embarrassed at having posted such a stark (and melodramatic) cry of pain on a Facebook page for anybody to see. But it had been seen already, and my phone rang a few minutes later.

Some months earlier, out on the "cat circuit," I'd struck up a friendship with Jackson Galaxy—Animal Planet's famous

and infamous "Cat Daddy"—and, as it turned out, he was every bit as compassionate in real life as one would expect from his show. He'd called now to see how Homer and I were doing, and I laid out my dilemma for him, sparing no details in describing Homer's recent visit to the animal hospital. I concluded by asking him the same question I'd been asking myself non-stop for days: Didn't I have to do something more for Homer—try some new doctor, some kind of medical treatment, *something* more than what I was doing?

Jackson listened until I'd talked myself out. "Homer is sending you a very clear message," he said when I'd finished. "And that message is *DO. NOT. WANT. I do not want this!* It's not fair to ignore a cat when he's talking to you that loudly and clearly."

"But how can I just do *nothing* for him?"

"Treating Homer with respect and dignity isn't nothing," Jackson told me. "Seeing him through this last phase of his life—however long that might be—with mindfulness and love isn't nothing." He paused for a moment, as if collecting his thoughts. "You have to be selfless now," he finally said. "You made an unspoken deal with Homer the day you adopted him. In loving him, you promised you'd always take care of him. Taking care of someone means putting them before you. And that means you, in this moment, don't matter. Your sadness doesn't matter. You'll have plenty of time for that when he leaves. In this moment, you're a parent with only one job. You have to listen to Homer, because the only promise to keep is not to wait until it's his worst day. Let him leave knowing love, not fear, not pain, not the flipside of love. Do you really want, *now*, to rob him of all that love and confidence he's had in such abundance his whole life?"

"No." My voice was husky. "No, I really don't."

"Just because doctors *can* do something doesn't mean they should. Just because you did certain things for your other cats doesn't mean you should do them for *this* cat. Every cat is different. You should follow Homer's lead."

"But Homer doesn't understand the choice he's making. He doesn't know what I know." I truly did want to let it go, to accept the reality of what was happening and make my peace with it. But the struggle had been too hard for me to give it up all at once.

"He knows what *he* knows. Maybe that's enough," Jackson concluded. "And Homer might end up surprising you. Cats usually do."

JACKSON'S WORDS PROVED to be prophetic. Days became weeks became months, and still Homer was with us. Still the same Homer more or less, although he did eventually slow a bit, like a clock just beginning to wind down.

The worst thing a cat can do for his liver is to stop eating—but, paradoxically, cats with liver disease are usually reluctant eaters at best. The challenge is to keep them eating, at least enough to give their liver something to do other than eat itself.

Homer, however, had always been a cat who defied expectations, and he ate voraciously. To say that Homer became a non-stop eating machine would be an understatement—and trying to describe what it was like to watch a four-pound cat eat his body weight every day is one of the rare times when words have failed me. It started with the medication the vet had prescribed, which

Laurence indulging Homer with prime rib

apparently was every bit as yummy as promised when mixed with his regular food. When the two weeks' worth of medication ran out, I made it my mission to keep the food party going. At first I started out with some kitten-hood favorites, long-since abandoned on health grounds— although my new philosophy was, *As long as he's eating and he's happy.* Kitten Chow once again became a permanent fixture in our cupboard, and Homer attacked it with so much zeal that it almost seemed as if eating the food he'd eaten when he was younger made him feel like a young cat again. Gooey cans of Friskie's and Fancy Feast also found their way into Homer's food bowl.

But it was Laurence who really rose to the occasion. What was, for me, a medical imperative became a genuine source of pleasure for Laurence, and finding new and exciting foods to tempt Homer with was his passion. That Homer was eating at all was less surprising than *how much* he was eating, consuming more than enough food in the typical day to satisfy a grown man.

Laurence brought Homer imported European canned tunas, sliced turkey by the pound, hamburgers, prime rib, shredded roast beef, pork-fried rice, spare ribs, pizza cheese, Gerber's baby food, and lobster dipped in butter. (The only thing Homer was particular about was his lobster—which was heaven on earth when dipped in butter, but unworthy of his interest when it was not.) He brought home salmon salad and whitefish salad from our favorite bagel place, and a stinky cheese from Murray's in the West Village that was so very stinky—even when stowed in the refrigerator—we'd had to ditch it a day later, even though the aroma had Homer clawing at the refrigerator door as if his very life depended on getting in.

Laurence's imagination ranged from the high to the low, and he also brought home mysterious "potted meats" found in fifty-cent cans at our local bodega, which Homer gobbled down as enthusiastically as if it were caviar (which Homer also grew to love during that final year). Cans of Vienna Sausages—again from our bodega—mashed with a fork and served *au jus* were a particular treat. Chinese chicken on the bone from the take-out place across the street was a big hit, although not nearly as tempting as a fried chicken breast from Popeye's, the smell of which drove Homer absolutely wild with delight. Homer could polish off an entire Popeye's breast in the space of half an hour, although perhaps Homer's greatest culinary accomplishment was the time he finished an entire mutton chop—literally bigger than he was!—that Laurence brought home from the legendary Keen's Steakhouse. (In fairness, I should add that it did take him two days to eat his way through the whole thing.) The image of little Homer, sitting in front of that giant mutton chop like a tiny Henry VIII about to dig into a palace banquet, is one I'll always be grateful to have in my memory.

Perhaps the only truly perplexing food that Homer developed a taste for was carrot cake. I'd brought home a slice without frosting from a health-food place, saving it as an after-dinner treat for myself. But a couple of hours later I found Homer on the kitchen counter, clawing off the plastic it was wrapped in and gobbling the cake down greedily. I was on the verge of stopping him—carrot cake striking me as an odd and potentially unhealthy choice for a cat. But then I thought, *why not?* and carried the rest to his bowl, for him to finish at his leisure.

It was clear to us that Homer was waging a tremendous battle, one that required an almost incomprehensible amount of fuel to keep it going. It seems to me now, looking back, that forgoing aggressive medical care turned out to be the right decision, if only because Homer would have fought it, and me, every step of the way. He almost certainly couldn't have battled on two fronts with nearly as much success as he battled now on just the one.

But even with all his strength—and I'll admit that I was a bit awed, this late in Homer's life, to realize fully just how tremendous that strength actually was—the battle was taking its toll. He napped far more than he used to, and lost weight until he was barely more than skin and bones. Running my hand down his back, I could feel every vertebra in his spine. His coat, once so lustrous and sleek, began to look oily. But as long as Homer still played and ate, as long as he still cuddled and purred and chased Fanny and Clayton around, I told myself that I would let him fight for his life on his own terms, without taking anything away from him.

Our bedroom became Homer's bedroom, and he slept with me every night. Whether because he was confused, or too tired to make the effort of jumping from the bed and walking to his litter-box (which I'd moved permanently into our bedroom), the bed became his nighttime litter-box during those last few months. Honesty compels me to add that those nighttime poops were…something—although who among us hasn't cleaned up that and worse while caring for an ailing cat? And, given both the size and nature of Homer's new daily diet, what else could be expected? Laurence moved temporarily into the guest bedroom, and I put a rubber sheet over our mattress. Stripping off all the sheets and blankets, I made a little nest for Homer from some of my old t-shirts and sweaters. As for myself, I slept wrapped up, cocoon-style, in a comforter. Homer and I were still able to cuddle, and it made clean-ups much easier.

I realize that, in the retelling, this sounds like an odd and cumbersome way to live—although it's amazing how quickly the unusual becomes routine when it's the landscape of your everyday life. I never thought of it as an imposition at all. I *wanted* to be there for all this—not just the playtimes and the cuddling, but the late-night cleanings and nursing Homer through bouts of upset stomach and every last messy, inconvenient bit of it. Once upon a time, I had saved Homer's life. And then, years later, he had saved mine. I can honestly say that I never loved Homer more than any of the other animals I've been lucky enough to live with. But Homer and I were bound to each other in a way that was nothing like anything I had experienced before—and I knew that I would never have anything in my life quite like this again. I couldn't have felt more tied to Homer if he'd literally been flesh of my flesh, bone of my bone.

When spring came, I resumed my schedule of shelter readings and fundraising appearances. Because I worked from home and spent, in the typical day, twenty-one hours or more within ten feet of Homer, it should have been easier to leave him once or twice a month for an afternoon trip upstate or a twenty-four-hour overnight to speak at a shelter farther away. Paradoxically, though, the more time I spent with Homer, the harder it was to go away from him. Still, talking about him at these events was a source of deep, deep pleasure.

People always asked about Homer during the Q&A sessions after I'd finished reading. Was he still alive? Was he in good health? I would tell the story of that last visit to the vet's office, how Homer—tiny Homer, sick as he was!—had overpowered the staff and thrown the entire animal hospital into disarray. I told them of the dire predictions that Homer wouldn't last out the month, wouldn't live to see the New Year. But here it was, the following summer, and Homer was still with us! A little slower, perhaps, and a little skinnier, but eating like a champ and enjoying his life.

People would shake their heads in astonishment. *How was such a thing possible? How could such a little cat have so much fight in him?* It became a standard part of these talks, of telling this story, for me to clench my right hand into a fist and strike the left side of my chest—just over my heart. In my best approximation of a Russian accent, I would proudly declare:

"Because my cat is strong like bull."

HOMER *WAS* STRONG like a bull—and he'd fought hard and far longer than any bull in a ring ever had. But it was a fight we'd always known couldn't go on forever.

The end came one late-August afternoon, nearly four years to the day since *Homer's Odyssey* had first been published. Laurence

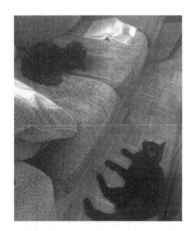

and I had gone out to run a few errands. When I walked back in through our front door, the first thing I saw was Homer hanging from the side of the couch, his front legs splayed out to full extension as he dangled from two claws—one in each front paw—that had become snagged in the fabric as he'd tried to pull himself up. Too exhausted to try very hard to free himself, he simply dangled, waiting mutely for me to find him and help.

Clayton keeping an eye on Homer

I'd noticed that Homer had slowed down even more in the past few days, that he'd gone from being tired to being *tired*, not stirring from his spot on the couch unless it was time for him to eat or follow me into the bedroom for the night. I'd also noticed that Clayton had seemed to be sticking to him more closely. Clayton was always fascinated by Homer and loved nothing more than to follow him around, even if Homer was ignoring him. But a sleeping Homer had never held much interest for Clayton, and when Homer settled down for a nap, Clayton would usually hop off to find something else to do. For the past week, though, whenever Homer curled up on the couch to sleep, Clayton would lie down on the floor directly in front of him—not moving, not bothering Homer in any way. He'd just watch him intently without taking his eyes off him.

I hadn't thought much about it at the time, and I'd tried not to think at all about Homer's increased weariness. On the face of it, there wasn't even a connection between those two things. But it all came together in my mind now in a single, blurred rush.

"Oh, *Homer.*" I threw down my purse and ran to the couch. "Oh, my poor boy. My poor, poor boy." I gently released the two claws and sank to the floor, cradling him in my arms, my cheek pressed to the top of his head. "I'm sorry, Homer-Bear. I'm so sorry I wasn't here. I'm so sorry, little boy." I swayed back and forth, kissing his brow, as he lay inertly in my arms. "I'm so sorry, Homer-Bear. I love you so much." I placed him on the ground, on his own legs. He feebly took a few steps, then laid down, clearly spent from the effort.

I went outside on our balcony then. Pulling the sliding door firmly closed behind me, I began to sob—great, gasping heaves that seemed to start at my knees before being wrenched upward and out through my mouth. I cried for having been gone when Homer needed me, and I felt the pain of that, his pain, as a physical pain in my own body. I cried for all the times I knew I would cry about it again, that image of Homer hanging from the couch. Countless times at unexpected moments, down through all the remaining years of my life. I cried for what I already knew in my heart even though I hadn't yet told it to myself in words. I cried for the blind kitten nobody had wanted, who'd come at a time in my life when I wasn't sure that anybody did, or ever would, want me. I cried for the last tangible link to those years of youth and uncertainty and discovery—a time that, even though it had since evolved into things infinitely better, was a vanished country now, one I could never return to. I cried for other things that would never come back, the greetings at the front door when I came home; the funny, sonar-like, sweeping turns of a little black head; the rattlesnake vibrating of an ecstatic tail (*Hooray! We're both here! We're together!*) that had been the first thing I'd seen every morning for sixteen years. I cried for all of it, although the only articulate word in my head was, *Never.* It was suddenly the only word in the whole world. An awful word. A final word. *Never. Never. Never.*

I had gone outside because I didn't want Homer to hear me cry like that, or Laurence for that matter. For their sakes, but also for my own. That first convulsion of grief was an animal thing, and instinctively I'd crawled away to hide my wound, to be alone with it. There was no one to hear me now but the buildings across the courtyard from ours. Their walls caught the sounds of my cries and sent them back to me, until the entire courtyard wailed in a Greek chorus of woe. *Alas! Alas!* I hung my head and arms over the balcony railing, pressing my hands over my eyes, and howled my loss to the empty courtyard below.

But I didn't allow myself to stay outside for more than a minute or two. I knew what had to be done, and I didn't want to give myself time to second-guess, to argue that maybe tomorrow would be better, that there might still be plenty of good days ahead. I had vowed that day when I'd spoken to Jackson, in preparation for just this moment, that I wouldn't wait until worse came to the absolute worst. I wouldn't wait until Homer wasn't Homer anymore before I let him go.

Months earlier, we'd found a vet who would be able to come to us at home when the time came. I had no intention of subjecting Homer to the animal hospital again, of making him spend the last moments of his life in the only place in the world of which he'd been starkly terrified. I spent the few hours before her arrival cuddling Homer in my lap and stroking his head in our old way. Laurence went out and got him a Popeye's chicken breast, which he mixed up with some turkey in Homer's bowl. Homer managed to make it from my lap as far as the bowl, but he was too tired to eat standing up and so ate reclining, like the Roman aristocrats of old. He did eat, though. He may not have cleaned his bowl, but he did eat.

The vet, when she came, was as kind as she'd sounded when I'd first spoken with her. She sat in the living room talking to Laurence and me about nothing in particular, until her presence among us stopped feeling awkward and ominous, and I was almost comfortable. Homer was lying in his spot at the end of the couch, close to her chair, and she affectionately stroked his head while she talked. He lay passively under her touch, although at one point he turned his head to press it into her hand.

Eventually, I picked Homer up and carried him into the bedroom, and the vet followed.

In the end, Homer died in his own home, in his own bed, in the arms of the person who'd loved him most. The vet left and quietly closed the bedroom door behind her after she'd given him the shot. I cradled Homer in my lap as I watched the muscles around the place where his eyes would have been relax into sleep for the last time. *"Eras mucho gato,"* I whispered into his ear. *Thou wert plenty of cat.*

It was, in its way, one of the most beautiful moments of my life. It was so beautiful that I couldn't even cry.

WHEN VASHTI DIED, we scattered her ashes at Fort Tryon Park, far, far uptown in Washington Heights. It was a beautiful, hilly park with acres of wide lawns and lush flowerbeds, and it commanded stunning views of the Hudson River and the Palisades beyond. Vashti had always loved water, and I had wanted to give her a whole river of it, a place from which she could watch the water sparkle and dance before it was carried out to sea. Scarlett had never shared Vashti's love of water and grass, but we had brought her ashes there too, so that she could be with Vashti.

And so, a week later, when we received Homer's ashes, we carried them all the way up to Fort Tryon Park, to the same lawn beneath the same oak tree where we'd released Scarlett and Vashti. My original three—Homer and his first, fastest friends—would be together again. The views were as sun-dappled and peaceful as I remembered. I hoped, I wanted to believe, that Homer at last was able to see them, to see all the beautiful things in this world that he never had, even though he'd seemed to be born knowing them already.

There was hardly anybody else at the park that day, and Laurence and I were alone in our little spot. I kissed the wooden box holding Homer's ashes before I opened it. As if awaiting its cue, a breeze blew up and carried them away from us, into the sunlight and out toward the river.

I wish I could say that I had a stirring eulogy for the occasion, something as heroic and fine as Homer himself had been. Something befitting the send-off of a cat who had touched so many lives, who had become the symbol of something so much bigger than himself, but who had never stopped being my own, my much-loved, dear little guy.

But I had expended so many words on Homer already—tens of thousands of them. My words were all used up. I could only think of someone else's. A scrap of an E.E. Cummings poem I'd first read back in my college creative-writing days, when I couldn't possibly have foreseen the little black cat who would find me someday and become the author of all my good fortune.

"I carry your heart with me," I said to the air and the ashes and the water flowing below us. "I carry it in my heart."

The breeze waned, and Homer's ashes, which had risen high above our heads, began to fall into the waiting grass. Laurence and I took each other's hands, and then we turned to go.

The End of the Beginning

Do not go about with your cheeks all covered with tears;
it is not right that you should grieve so incessantly.

-HOMER, *The Odyssey*

I WAITED NEARLY A WEEK BEFORE I LET HOMER'S ONLINE COMMUNITY know about his passing, needing time to mourn privately before I could do so publicly. I had known that the response would be overwhelming, although I didn't know then how overwhelming it would be. The news about Homer grew and spread and then grew more, changing our lives and Homer's legacy in ways we could never have imagined.

But before I write about any of that, the time has come, as promised, to write about Clayton and Fanny—how we adopted them, what they brought to our family, and what they came to mean to us. The last chapter of Homer's story is very much their story, too.

WHEN I SET out to find a kitten to adopt as a companion for Homer, it was the first time I'd adopted a cat with a specific list of "qualifications" in mind. Actually, it was the first time I'd deliberately set out to adopt a cat at all. Homer, Vashti, and Scarlett had all come into my life through a fortuitous combination of luck and circumstances and—while not generally a superstitious person—I'd believed in the karmic destiny of that, the sense that the cats I had been meant to love had found me, rather than vice versa. This was true even of the two older cats we'd tried out previously with Homer. And while things hadn't worked out permanently with our fosters, at least I'd been able to save them from certain death and help them find loving forever homes. Maybe that also was fate at work.

Now, however, we were looking for a kitten—not just waiting for one, but *looking*, because what Homer desperately needed after losing Scarlett was someone aside from Laurence and me to keep him company. The kitten ideally would still be very young—no older than two or three months, say—so that he or she would accept Homer's unusual face and particular ways without knowing that "normal" adult cats looked or acted any differently. I felt that we were uniquely suited to give a home to a kitten who had special needs. And, I soon realized, if we were going to adopt *one* young kitten, we should probably adopt *two*. Kittens were high energy, and a kitten with no one to play with besides Homer might drive him to distraction.

I entered my search parameters on Petfinder.com, and after a few clicks found myself looking at a picture of two kittens named Peeta and Katniss. They were a bonded pair of litter-mates with a foster network called Forever Friends—located deep in South Jersey, only an hour-and-a-half away by train—who hoped to adopt the two of them out together. Both kittens were entirely black, although Katniss had a little locket of white fur just above her breastbone.

Peeta had a deformed hind leg, more of a half-leg, really, which would likely have to come off at some point when he was older than the ten weeks he currently was. It didn't reach more than halfway to the ground and was of no use in propelling him forward when he walked, but he nonetheless uselessly spun and spun the half-leg as he moved, wasting energy and risking injury.

I knew as soon as I saw them that these were our kittens. The sun hadn't even come up yet when I filled out the online application, and I waited in a keyed-up state of anticipation for the hours to roll by until it was late enough for a (ahem) sane person to begin their workday and review the form I'd submitted. I received a call from Forever Friends before noon, and we talked for a while about Peeta and Katniss, their personalities, Peeta's special needs. I gave them a list of references, and a week later I stood on the platform of New Jersey Transit's Trenton station, waiting to meet the volunteer from Forever Friends who would deliver our newest family members.

Laurence and I had enjoyed the *Hunger Games* movies well enough, but ultimately wanted to name the kittens ourselves. Laurence chose Clayton for the boy, after the famous one-legged tap dancer Clayton "Peg Leg" Bates. I chose Fanny for the girl, simply because I thought it was a sweet, old-fashioned name, and in her pictures Katniss looked like a very sweet little girl.

WHEN FANNY AND Clayton came to us, it had been fifteen years since I'd lived with a kitten—and I'd never lived with litter-mates at all. I was charmed to see what a matched set they were, how they groomed each other lovingly and slept curled up in each other's bodies. Their faces had enough subtle differences to be distinguishable, yet the family resemblance was obvious. They had identical large, golden eyes, and a habit of sitting next to each other with their heads tilted at identical angles, regarding Laurence and me with identical wide-eyed, solemn gazes. It was adorable, yet at times could take on an almost eerie, *Children of the Corn* quality.

The most enduring early image I have of the two of them comes from the evening of their fourth day with us. We'd set them up in our guest bedroom at first, wanting to give them a chance to acclimate, to feel safe in their new space and to get used to things smelling like Homer, while also giving Homer a chance to get used to things—like the t-shirts I let them sleep on and then wore around the house—smelling like them.

On the fourth day, I opened the door to the guest room and let them out into the rest of the apartment for the first time. Clayton, as if shot from a cannon, immediately took off in a quick bunny-hop on his three good legs, down the long hallway and into the living room. Fanny, however, stood anxiously in the doorway to the guest room, crying for her brother to come back. Every few minutes, Clayton would hop back down the hall to where Fanny stood, touching his nose to hers in a reassuring way. *Come on! There's lots of cool stuff to explore out here!* But he was too eager to see his new home to remain with her for long, and soon enough he'd scamper away again.

Much of what we came to learn about their personalities was reflected in those few minutes. Fanny was a fawn-like creature—timid at first, easily spooked, but essentially composed of such pure sweetness and affection that it was like having Vashti with us again. It should be noted, however, that in terms of appearance, Fanny was Vashti's exact inverse. Where Vashti had been a puffy white fluff-ball, Fanny's black, short-haired body grew long and slender as it took on the contours of adulthood. But she was, in her precisely opposite way, every inch the beauty Vashti had been. I liked to say that Fanny's face looked as if it had been drawn by Disney

Princess animators, perfectly heart-shaped with high cheekbones, a slightly pointed chin, and tip-tilted almond eyes. "You're so pretty," Laurence would croon to her when he thought I couldn't hear. "You're a pretty, *pretty* girl." And, like Vashti before her, Fanny would lean her head into Laurence's hand and gaze up at him

Fanny, circa 2013

adoringly. Perhaps because Fanny was so Vashti-like in so many of her ways, she and Laurence seemed to understand each other right from the start.

Fanny seemed to understand Homer immediately, too. She was intensely interested in him once she'd made it out of the guest room, but she always approached him gently and respectfully. She would wait until he'd finished cautiously sniffing her and seemed comfortable before attempting to touch her own nose softly to his. If Homer batted a crumpled ball of paper around the living room floor, she would bat it back to him but not otherwise try to intrude on his game until he'd come over and explicitly invited her to play. If Homer curled up on the couch, Fanny would also lie on the couch close enough to make Homer aware that he wasn't alone, but not so close as to make him feel crowded.

I don't think she understood that Homer was blind, per se, but she seemed to intuit that he was happiest when he could hear her coming. We'd bought belled breakaway collars for the kittens for just this reason. But Fanny always greeted Homer with a trilling coo, as an additional assurance that her approach was both imminent and friendly. As weeks passed and Homer began to revert to his former playful ways—to once again seek out mischief and fun and food as eagerly as he'd used to—it became clear that this was, at least in part, because Fanny was a balm on the wound that Scarlett's loss had left on Homer's spirit.

Clayton, on the other hand, was an intrepid little soul, ready of an instant to bound fearlessly and inquisitively at anything or anyone that crossed his path. Clayton darted down the hallway the day we opened the guest-room door for him, and he never stopped darting, never stopped exploring, never stopped trying to insert himself into everything going on around him. If I'd thought that Homer lacked even a concept of vision because he himself was unable to see, then Clayton seemed to lack even the idea that anyone might not like him, simply because he himself was utterly incapable of disliking anybody or anything.

I'll admit that Clayton was a puzzle to me for a long time. To say that cats are highly opinionated creatures is almost as reflexively obvious as saying that they have fur and whiskers. Even the most agreeable cat will have certain strong likes and dislikes. Fanny, for example, adored little toy mice and anything with feathers, but wasn't much interested in any other toys. She was passionate about cat foods made from lamb, duck, or tuna, but couldn't abide anything containing salmon or beef. As good-natured as Homer was, he hated being picked up, loathed being turned on his back, and would instantly recoil if you laid so much as a finger on his belly.

But Clayton liked everything. Literally *everything*. He liked crinkle balls and feathered toys and little fake mice and the plastic rings from water jugs and matchbooks and eyeglass cases and takeout menus and anything else small or portable enough for him to carry off in his mouth. He would eat anything you put in front of him. Dry or moist, regardless of flavor or texture—he ate everything and ate it all with equal gusto. You could pick him up, flip him over, rub his tummy, handle him however you liked, and he would nuzzle your hand and ask for more. One afternoon he sat in a chair with Laurence's visiting ten-year-old nephew, who (only for not knowing any better) spent nearly half an hour rubbing Clayton's fur the wrong way, while Clayton closed his eyes in a drowsy half-sleep, entirely unruffled.

Clayton liked everybody who came to our home and bunny-hopped out to greet them as fast as his three legs could carry him. He had a thick, club-like tail that swung out like a rudder at skewed angles behind him as he ran, most likely to compensate for some of the balance he lacked. When he wasn't running, however, his tail seemed stuck permanently in a happy, upward thrust, guaranteeing anyone who approached a friendly—a downright enthusiastic—reception.

Clayton even liked the vet. *He liked the vet!* A little cut at the bottom of his bad leg became infected and wouldn't heal, requiring the removal of that leg months ahead of our original schedule. There were a number of vet visits leading up to the surgery—and then the surgery itself—and Clayton not only didn't struggle or complain, he actually seemed to *enjoy* himself. When the vet pried back Clayton's lips to examine his gums and teeth, Clayton purred ecstatically. When the doctor stuck a needle into him to draw blood, Clayton butted his forehead playfully into the crook of the doctor's elbow. When he poked gingerly at the bottom of Clayton's infected half-leg—which, surely, must have been at least a little painful—Clayton flipped onto his back and bonked his whole head affectionately against the doctor while licking his hand. I couldn't help but feel somewhat vindicated at entering the same animal hospital where Homer had always caused such a ruckus with a *good* patient for a change.

But still…I wondered about things.

Fanny, as she grew, began to develop an adult cat's more complex vocal patterns—perhaps not as varied as Homer's, but deeper and more mature sounding than when she'd been only a few weeks old. Clayton, however, still had a very young kitten's undifferentiated, high-pitched squeak. His *meow* didn't even have an "ow" at the end. *"MEEEEEEEEeeee,"* he would say, starting out loud but trailing off as his breath ran out. *"MEEEEEEEEeeee,"* he said when I walked in the door, and, *"MEEEEEEEEeeee,"* he said when he wanted his food, and, *"MEEEEEEEEeeee,"* running to greet some new person, and, *"MEEEEEEEEeeee,"* when struggling for a plaything that was out of his reach. I joked that when the doctors had removed his bad leg, they'd taken away his "ow."

"There isn't any sign of…neurological damage, is there?" I asked the vet during one visit, just before Clayton's surgery. "Any developmental delays?"

He seemed baffled. "What do you mean? Like brain damage?"

"No," I said hastily. "Never mind. Just forget it."

Of course, Clayton was our veterinary practice's favorite cat, and whenever we came in there was a veritable welcoming committee waiting for us at the door. What a dream for a veterinarian—who presumably liked cats, yet only encountered cats who feared him—to finally find a cat who seemed positively thrilled in his presence. And what a dream for Clayton—who happily scamper-hopped around the exam table from the doctor to the vet tech and back again, demanding cuddles with a head-bonk and a high-pitched *MEEEEEEEEeeee,* hardly seeming aware of the needles, the rectal thermometer, or any of the other indignities to which he was subjected.

Perhaps the only thing Clayton didn't like was not having anyone around for him to like. It wasn't so much that he feared or disliked being alone. He simply never needed to be. Even Homer— much as he generally preferred to be with me—would *sometimes* head off to any empty bedroom or open closet. Fanny, sweet as she was and as much as she clearly loved us already, needed at least a few hours a day by herself, and would always prefer to be hidden away in some quiet spot when we had people over.

But Clayton never wanted to be alone, or even out of plain sight. Clayton didn't nap on top of chairs or under beds or buried among piles of clothing or tucked away in a corner of the closet.

He'd sprawl out smack-dab in the middle of the floor of whatever room we were in, where you couldn't walk from one end of the room to the other without stepping over him. A question that, to this day, has literally never once been asked in our home is, *Where's Clayton? I haven't seen Clayton in a while.*

As I said, I loved Clayton right from the start—but he puzzled me. Part of the bond that we form with the animals we love comes from that sense that they know us, and that we know them, better than anybody else does or could. I never had—and never would—understand anybody down to the very bottom of their soul the way that I did Homer. I knew every like and dislike, every joy and fear, that Homer had, and had felt the first glimmers of that deep knowledge in those very earliest moments when we'd first met.

But what did I know about Clayton that any stranger couldn't have figured out within five minutes? What ultimately makes all of us different from each other—different and unique—are the things we like and the things we don't. Clayton liked everything and disliked nothing—or, if he did, he kept it to himself—which made him a bit inscrutable.

But if there was one thing that Clayton definitively liked more than anything else—one thing that could raise his usual level of happiness to outright ecstasy—that thing was Homer. Small as Homer was, he still towered over Clayton when we first adopted him—and Clayton clearly thought that Homer was the most fascinating thing in the whole world.

Clayton wasn't much interested in Homer when Homer was sleeping. But if Homer was awake and in motion then Clayton was right beside him. When Homer walked to his food bowl or the litter-box or down the hall, Clayton bunny-hopped along at his side. The pushiness of this—the lack of any respect for polite boundaries—irritated Homer at first. Every few steps, Homer would pause to whack Clayton in the face with one paw.

I don't know that Clayton *liked* being hit in the face by

Homer, but it didn't seem to faze him, either. He'd crinkle his little brow a bit, but he never flinched or stepped back or raised his own small paw in a gesture of self-defense. He'd hop next to Homer or around him in circles, and every few feet Homer would pause to smack him in the face—and, like a Slinky, Clayton's head and neck would compress for a moment, then instantly spring back up.

Homer and Clayton together reminded me of Spike the Bulldog and Chester the Terrier from the old Looney Tunes cartoons. Spike would stride impressively down the sidewalk with little Chester scampering around him, peppering him with an endless stream of eager questions. *What are you doing, Spike? What are doing today? Where are you going, Spike? Huh? Can I come with you, Spike? Can I?* And every so often, without breaking stride, Spike would whack Chester in the face with a laconic, *Ehhh...shut up.*

That was Homer and Clayton to a T.

It pained me to see Homer bothered in any way, after the rough few months he'd had. But, ultimately, being irritated with Clayton was better than being sad about Scarlett. Homer began running and jumping again, at first to avoid Clayton, and then simply for the pleasure of it, as he'd used to do. If Fanny charmed and soothed him, then Clayton brought him out of his shell.

Scarlett and Vashti had never been as playful as Homer would have liked, and with them he'd never been able to assume a role more authoritative than that of mildly annoying little brother. Now Homer was the big brother, accompanied by two kittens who loved to play as much as he did and then some. He had reasons to get up from his spot on the couch, other than feeding times or his daily shift from the sofa to my lap. Clayton and Fanny were perfectly content to be minions and let Homer be the boss, and it was a role that Homer clearly relished.

Even if I hadn't been able to love them for their own sakes (and I was crazy about them—they were, as I would frequently say to Laurence, "made of adorable"), I would have loved Fanny and Clayton for bringing Homer back to me—*my* Homer, the Homer I knew and loved best, the Homer who'd always greeted each new day as something to celebrate. Homer was *Homer* again.

And I honestly believe that Homer wouldn't have found the strength he needed to fight his illness for as long as he did if not for these two ridiculously happy little ragamuffins, who moved into our home and claimed our lives for themselves.

HOMER HAD SOMETHING like fifteen thousand followers on Twitter, but it was on Facebook and my blog where his real community lived. By now, there were nearly thirteen thousand people who'd "liked" Homer's Facebook page, but the number of people who actually followed us there on a day-to-day basis was still very small. They were the people for whom I posted pictures of Clayton and Fanny as they grew, and who had sincerely mourned with us when we'd lost our girls.   Homer's community gave us the permission and space we needed to embrace our grief fully and recover at our own pace, without having to encounter a single person who rolled their eyes and wondered rather impatiently why we couldn't get over it already—why we were so sad when it was "just a cat."

I had known that the grief would be deeper, the sense of loss more profound, when we lost Homer. It was Homer's community, after all.   But I had thought—naively, I now realize—that it would be more or less a slightly larger version of the same thing. Thinking this—that the one or two hundred comments and emails of condolence we had received after losing Vashti and Scarlett might be as many as four or five hundred now—I had waited four days after Homer's passing, enough time to put on a "game face," before posting the announcement to social media. It was August 25th— as fate would have it (although I didn't register this at the time), exactly four years to the day since *Homer's Odyssey* had first been published in 2009.

Publishing Homer's story had changed my life, but that change had been a slow one—because book publishing is a slow business. I'd spent nearly a year writing the proposal and outline for *Homer's Odyssey*, another year finding a publisher and then writing the book itself, and it had been six months after *that* before the book had first appeared in hardcover. Even all the craziness of Homer's photo and video shoots had played out over a period of months, turning our lives topsy-turvy for perhaps one day every two or three weeks, and then leaving us to enjoy relative normalcy the rest of the time.

Nothing at all in my previous experience had prepared me for what it felt like to have my whole life change in a day.

The Facebook post announcing Homer's death was shared more than three thousand times, and received more than eight thousand comments, within only the first few hours. People began posting pictures and stories of their own special-needs rescue animals to Homer's page—animals they said they had been inspired to adopt by Homer's example. Most of them were cats—cats large and small, fluffy and hairless, former street cats, backyard cats, cats who had been considered "undesirable" by their breeders. Cats who were blind or deaf or both, or who were missing limbs or paralyzed from the waist down. "Wobbly" cats suffering from cerebellar hypoplasia, and cats who were positive for FIV or FeLV. There were also many special-needs dogs, a handful of rescued bunnies and horses, and one albino gecko with poor depth perception. (I swear I'm not making that up.)

I shared these pictures and stories with Homer's community as they came in, thinking them the most fitting tribute Homer could possibly have received. But for every one story and picture I shared, three or four more would appear in the "Visitor Posts" column along the side of the page, until I could no longer keep up. And people posted other things, too. They found older pictures of Homer that I'd posted online years earlier, and they shared them again on

Homer's page now. Sometimes they Photoshopped these pictures, to give Homer angels' wings, to show him at the Rainbow Bridge, to frame him with solemn black borders that announced the years of his birth and his death. Each photo and post moved me deeply—until a few days later, when the numbers were so large that I was simply bewildered. I hadn't known there were so many. I'd had no idea.

Facebook's algorithms clearly interpreted this influx of new activity on our page as "good," and began sending more and more and then even *more* traffic our way. It had taken nearly four years for Homer's page to accumulate those thirteen thousand "likes," to reach a point where content from the page reached perhaps five thousand people in a week. I had thought those numbers were pretty big. But, within a week of Homer's death, his page had acquired an additional fourteen thousand followers and reached more than two million people. Hour by hour, day by day, Laurence and I watched those numbers go up, thinking every day that surely—*surely*—today was the day when it would all begin to level off.

And every day we thought that, we were wrong.

When you lose a member of your human family, there's usually one day when you reach out to all the people who need to be called or notified, and then that part is done. But social media doesn't work that way. For all the thousands of people who'd seen my Facebook post within hours of its going up, there were many thousands more who didn't first see it in their news feeds for another day, or several days, or a couple of weeks. Every day there were people who were only now first seeing their friend's re-tweet of somebody else's Twitter post that had gone up days ago. Every day somebody visited my website—not even knowing there was any specific news about Homer—and, reading my blog post for the first time, then forwarded it to half a dozen other people they knew, who themselves forwarded the link to a dozen more. Every day, somebody saw for the first time the share, re-tweet, or re-post of another blogger's tribute to Homer.

Sometimes the news was divorced from social media altogether—a rumor that people heard word-of-mouth, and they wrote to me for confirmation. At least twenty or thirty times in the typical day, I would receive emails from people wanting to know if what they'd heard was true, if Homer was really gone, and if so, when and how had it happened?

For me, every day was the first day all over again. I felt like a skipping record, forced to keep repeating the same notes over and over because my needle was stuck in a groove and couldn't get unstuck.

Laurence has never said so, but I suspect that I wasn't exactly the world's greatest wife during this time. I know now that Fanny, and especially Clayton, felt a difference in me, too. I petted and played with them as much as I ever had, but something essential within me was becoming numbed.

The emails began pouring in immediately after I posted that first announcement, and within a few days they were followed by sympathy cards in the mail—first in a trickle, then in a gush, like something out of *Miracle on 34th Street*. We received hundreds—literally hundreds—of sympathy cards and letters, and hundreds more cards from shelters and rescue groups, informing us of donations that had been made in Homer's name. Along with the cards and letters, people sent us their own home-made versions of Homer—stuffed macramé Homers, ceramic Homers, Homers blown from black glass, a watercolor painting of Homer from Brazil, a Homer necklace pendant carved out of an old vinyl record from San Francisco, a hand-painted sculpture depicting a super-hero-caped Homer in front of the Twin Towers from Iowa, a soft-sculpture Homer purse that came all the way from Japan, a framed Homer needlepointed in black Egyptian silk and surrounded by gold thread from Los Angeles, and even an extravagantly framed oil portrait of Homer from "Hank For Senate's" humans in Virginia. Soon the media inquiries followed. I ended up asking a book publicist I'd worked with once to write up a press release containing the essential facts and some boilerplate quotes from me, so that inquiring press could have something to work with without my having to tell the same story dozens of times. A few months later, *The New York Times Magazine* would run Homer's obituary online as part of December's annual "The Lives They Lived" feature, which rounded up notable deaths from the preceding year. By then, enough time had passed for me to be proud and even a little amused, to wryly observe to Laurence that we certainly shouldn't expect the same kind of coverage when our time came.

But, at the time these things were happening, all I could think when dealing with press was that I was afraid of repeating the same things too often and sounding like a robot, yet also afraid of deviating from my stock answers and sounding like a moron.

I know how I sound in writing all this. *How awful it must have been for you, to receive the heartfelt love and sympathy of so many people!* It wasn't awful at all, of course. It was astounding, amazing, miraculous enough to convince even the most hard-hearted cynic of the generosity and infinite kindness people were capable of.

Every time somebody wrote to say that they felt as if Homer had been their own cat—that they'd cried upon hearing the news as if they'd lost one of their own—my own heart throbbed in sympathy. I knew—I *knew*—exactly how that felt. When I saw all the donations that had been made in Homer's name and thought of the lives that would be saved because of them, my heart swelled with gratitude. When I received all the beautiful things people made and sent to us, I was thankful until I thought my heart would burst with it.

And that was the problem—there was too much to feel and not enough me to feel it all. My life already felt strange and unlike my own life simply because Homer was no longer in it. But now, when I woke up, I would spend a good couple of hours walking around in a daze, not knowing how to pick up the thread of the day, where I should start, who I should call, which emails and inquiries and Facebook posts I was supposed to respond to.

Once my days had flowed along a natural, effortless rhythm that I didn't have to think about. Now I spent a half-hour each morning trying to decide when to take a shower. Did it make more sense to do a little work, then shower, and then get back to work again? Or would it be more logical and efficient to shower immediately, before I did anything else? Half the time I ended up not showering at all. Better to avoid the question altogether, I'd sagely conclude, rather than come up with the wrong answer.

I eventually realized that Laurence had seamlessly taken over most of the essential tasks that kept our lives running. It was Laurence who now fed Clayton and Fanny on their regular schedule. He also cleaned their litter-box, trimmed their claws, and fished their toys out from under the couch. Laurence prepared our meals and made sure I ate, kept us stocked with toilet paper and trash bags and toothpaste, wrote out checks for bills and made sure they were mailed on time.

All the gratitude, all the love, all the sorrow for the pain of others that I felt, overloaded me until all I felt was overwhelmed— overwhelmed and anxious, slipping further behind each day on all the thank-yous and acknowledgments I owed people, which continued to accumulate in new batches by the hour.

Somewhere, underneath this giant mound of *stuff* that had amassed atop me, was my grief for Homer. I had written about it, blogged about it, emailed Homer's mourners about it. But sometime in the midst of all that, at some point after we'd scattered his ashes and there was no physical, tangible task left for me to do, I'd lost my ability to feel it.

What I needed was to cry. I hadn't cried at all since that first wild convulsion of loss on the afternoon of the night when Homer had gone to sleep for the last time. Now I needed to shed the gentler tears of letting go. I had to get back to my grief in order to heal from it and move on.

But I couldn't. I couldn't find it. I didn't remember ever having felt as tired as I did now. I was too exhausted even to look.

MY OWN LIFE had been turned inside out, but as far as I could tell Clayton and Fanny were as happy as they'd ever been. They still ate big meals and napped together in sunbeams, still chased crinkle balls and the laser pointer's ever-elusive red dot with the same joyous abandon. When I piled all the sympathy cards and letters we'd received into the middle of the living room rug—hoping to create some semblance of order from them—Clayton would dive right into the middle of the pile, burrowing into and under it as if he were a child in a ball tank.

It was a few weeks later, in late September, when I noticed one evening that Clayton was having trouble with his litter-box, hopping in and out of it more frequently than was usual. When I checked, however, he didn't seem to be producing anything. I assumed that he was a little blocked, and I added some olive oil to his moist food for an evening meal. He gobbled the whole thing down with his typical enthusiasm, which I found reassuring.

Later that night, however, it was a different story. Clayton was in and out of his litter-box every few minutes now, his pupils hugely dilated. When he wasn't in the litter-box, he paced back and forth across the living room in an odd fashion, crouching first in one random spot, then another.

I had been planning to take him to his regular vet the next morning if the problem persisted. But he seemed so *very* uncomfortable—and was acting in so very unusual a way—that I didn't want to make him wait another eight hours for relief. If it had been Homer, who'd hated the vet with a furious passion, I might have taken a more wait-and-see attitude. But Clayton didn't mind doctors, and even though it was 11:00 and our animal clinic was closed for the night, I thought, *Better safe than sorry.* So, bundling him into his carrier, and waiting for Laurence to grab a jacket so he could accompany us as far as the sidewalk and see us safely into a cab, I headed for the 24-hour emergency animal hospital on West Fifteenth Street.

The last time I'd been in a cab ferrying a cat to an emergency room had been with Homer, and that had clearly been a life-or-death situation. It didn't feel like that this time, though. I still believed the problem was constipation—albeit clearly a severe case—because, in my range of experience with cat maladies, I hadn't yet encountered anything else that seemed to match these symptoms. Vashti's CRF had caused her to be constipated from time to time, and Clayton's behavior now wasn't completely dissimilar to what hers had been then.

Vashti's physical inverse, Fanny, may have been sleek and slender, but Clayton was mushy in the middle. He was a bit of a food hound, and had a habit— one we couldn't break—of finishing his own meals and then tackling Fanny's. Fanny was always obliging enough to allow him to do so. She was a healthy weight, according to her doctor, and even when I'd secretly put

Clayton, auditioning to be the new plus-sized Puma logo

down some extra food for her when Clayton wasn't looking, she didn't seem particularly interested. So I assumed now that Clayton had eaten too much of something that didn't agree with him, and my heart ached with sympathy for his obvious discomfort. I reached my hand through the top of his cloth carrier to stroke his head reassuringly. *Poor kitty,* I crooned. *Poor Clayton.* But I also murmured, with a kind of rough affection, *Maybe now you'll learn your lesson, and let poor Fanny eat her meals in peace.*

The emergency animal hospital on West Fifteenth was the polar opposite of our regular clinic—a cavernous, fluorescent-lit waiting area studded with row after row of hard-backed chairs. It was close to midnight, and the only other person in the enormous space was a man with a huge German Shepherd, who'd just finished being sick all over the spotless linoleum floor. Another man in a blue orderly's uniform hurried over with a mop and push-bucket, while the man with the dog patted his flank in a soothing way, helping him into an exam room in the back. The woman at the check-in desk took Clayton's name, the reason for our visit, and my credit card information with brisk efficiency. We didn't have to wait more than a few minutes before a doctor approached and summoned us into an exam room of our own.

Clayton didn't struggle as the vet lifted him from his carrier, but he did mewl in a pained, pathetic way when her hands first went under his belly for support, then gently probed his lower abdomen. I couldn't remember ever hearing Clayton make a sound that wasn't *happy.* And, for the first time, I felt the stirrings of fear in my own belly.

"Have you noticed any blood in his urine?" she asked.

"No." The question startled me. *His urine?* "You don't think it's constipation?"

She removed the little blanket lining Clayton's carrier and spread it onto the exam table, so that Clayton could lie down more comfortably. "I think he has something called feline idiopathic cystitis," she said. "It's a blockage of the urinary tract. It's life-threatening if we don't catch it in time, although," she hastily assured me, "it's highly treatable when we do. We call it 'idiopathic' because we don't really know what causes the condition. Generally we think it's brought on by stress. Have there been any significant changes in your home recently?"

At first, the combination of the words *stress* and *Clayton* in the same sentence struck me as so absurd that it was almost comical. Was any cat ever *less* prone to stress than Clayton was?

But then, unbidden, a memory came back to me. When the vet had come to us on Homer's last day, she'd wrapped him in a blanket when it was over, leaving only his face revealed. She'd then placed his body tenderly in a bag she'd brought with her—a roomy leather bag with handles.

The bag containing Homer had remained opened and unzipped on the floor while I signed papers and made arrangements for the cremation. And Clayton had climbed into it. I'd thought it merely the natural curiosity of any cat to explore an open bag left on the floor. But, when we'd tried to lift him out, Clayton had clung to the blanket around Homer, whining anxiously as we'd fought to pull him away.

Grief has a way of making us selfish. As many people as had mourned for Homer—and as sincere and deep as I'd known that mourning to be—I'd been sure that nobody's loss could equal my own. Homer had been *my* cat, his loss had been *my* loss—and there was no one, I thought, who could truly know how I felt.

Clayton lay on the exam table between the doctor and me, the gold of his eyes dulled from their usual bright alertness. But when I placed my hand down on the table next to him, he laid one small, black paw over it and looked up into my face.

I had been wrong. There *had* been another who'd known how I felt. Someone else had felt his happily ordered world run off course, had lost his hero and very best friend, not understanding *why* that friend was gone and couldn't come back to play with him anymore.

He just hadn't known how to tell me.

My voice was gritty when I spoke. "Our oldest cat…" The words stuck, and I realized that, for all the blogs and emails and Facebook posts, I hadn't actually said it aloud to anyone. Not once.

Not in all this time.

I cleared my throat and tried again. "Our oldest cat died a few weeks ago. Clayton was very attached to him."

I felt the relief of saying it—just saying it as a commonplace statement, to a person who didn't know Homer or that I was "Homer's mom," who would greet the idea with nothing more than ordinary, professional sympathy—pass through me. It felt like having a rusty gate you'd been pushing and pushing against finally begin to swing open, just a crack.

"I'm so sorry," the vet said. "That could certainly do it."

"But Clayton will…" I cleared my throat a second time. "He will be okay, right? I did get him here in time?" *Not again,* I thought. *Please not again, not now, not so soon…*

"I think he'll be fine," she replied. "He'll have to stay with us for two or three days so we can clear the blockage and get everything flowing the way it should. Let me take him back now and get him started. You can wait up front for the receptionist to bring the papers you'll need to sign."

CLAYTON WAS AWAY for three days. I'd always gone to visit our other cats when they'd had overnight hospital stays. When Clayton had his leg removed, I'd seen him at least once a day. He'd had to stay for two weeks then, so he could be crated while his stitches healed. It was impossible to imagine otherwise how we would have kept a rambunctious kitten stable enough not to risk the stitches—or how we would have kept Fanny, who groomed him daily, from going after them herself. Keeping Clayton crated at home—in full view of the rest of us interacting with each other, but not with him—had seemed unnecessarily torturous. But I'd gone to see him every afternoon and brought him treats. And the doctor and other staff members had taken him periodically into an empty exam room for brief bouts of closely supervised play. He'd seemed nothing but happy when I'd visited him then, surrounded by toys that he batted around playfully when he was in his cage, and by adoring humans during the brief times he was allowed out of it. This time, however, the hospital asked that I not come and visit. It was important that Clayton remain hooked up to tubes and catheters around the clock, and unhooking him long enough for a visit from me was, I was told, an undesirable option. I called three times each day to check on him, and at a minimum I knew that Clayton was still the easy patient, as compliant with staff as he'd always been. The day when I finally went to bring him home, a tech handed over his carrier and informed me, "Clayton is the most adorablest cat ever." Which told me that his usual sunny charm must have returned during those three days, at least in part.

I was given a sheet with after-care instructions, a case of a new prescription food, and a bill so steep that I almost reeled. (An emergency animal hospital in Manhattan possibly being the most expensive option for veterinary care anywhere on the planet.) It was worth it, though, as I saw Clayton's soft carrier pop like popcorn when he heard my voice, and realized that I had come back for him.

Clayton was overjoyed to be released from that carrier once we got home—although taken aback by Fanny's hostile reception. He may have *looked* like the Clayton she knew, but he *smelled* like something else altogether, and Fanny backed up and hissed at him angrily whenever he approached. I quickly brought Clayton into our bedroom, which I'd set up ahead of time with a new litter-box, his favorite toys and blankets, and a bowl for his new food. If stress had caused his illness, I didn't want his recovery set back by the additional stress of rejection. Within a few days, I knew, Clayton would smell like himself again, and he and Fanny could fall back into their established patterns of close companionship.

Laurence came in every so often to check on us, and Clayton scampered over to bonk his head joyously against Laurence's hand as he bent down to scratch behind Clayton's ears. *Look! I'm back! I'm finally home!* But otherwise Clayton and I were alone together for the rest of the night. He bunny-hopped frenetically around the bedroom for a long time, thrilled to be released from the confinement of the hospital, delighted to reacquaint himself with his favorite toys, which he chased with dizzying speed over and under the bed, from one end of the room to the other. Every few minutes he'd jump into his litter-box, releasing a few small dribbles each time, which would have alarmed me if his doctor hadn't told me to expect this for a day or two.

It was late by the time he'd finally exhausted himself. Switching off the bedside lamp, I crawled beneath the covers and readied myself for sleep. I'd set up a soft pile of blankets and pillows on the floor for Clayton, as he'd never really been a cuddler or expressed much interest in sharing our bed. As friendly as he could be, Clayton wasn't a lap cat. If I sat on the floor, he'd hop around me in counter-clockwise circles, bumping his head affectionately against my shoulder or back as he went, pausing on occasion to rest in my lap for the briefest of seconds before leaping up and resuming his bunny-hop circles.

I'd never expected that any of our cats would cuddle on demand—Scarlett would certainly have disabused me of any such notion a long time ago. Still, one of the things I missed most about Homer was no longer having a furry little body to curl up with. I missed that feeling of peace that comes only when a small animal trusts you enough to fall asleep in your arms.

So it surprised me, as I got under the blankets, when Clayton climbed onto the bed after me. And then he did something he'd never done before. Hopping across the bed to where I lay, he nosed the covers aside and stretched his body across mine, one hind leg tucked beneath my right arm, while his front paws sprawled out to touch my left. His chest was directly over my chest, his heart aligned with my own. My arms rose from the bed to embrace him, and Clayton nuzzled his nose into my neck, purring gently against my left ear.

It was then—at last, at long last—that my tears began to flow. Not the harsh animal sobs of the day I'd lost Homer, but something infinitely softer than that, an easing, a warm, fluid salt. Clayton's weight was heavy on my chest, and yet it felt lighter than it had in weeks, as if it were emptying out as the tears ran down my cheeks. They mingled with Clayton's black fur as he brought his head to mine and, with exquisite patience, licked the tears from my skin with his raspy tongue, as the soft thrum of his purrs rumbled against my ear.

Baby boy, I whispered. *My little baby boy.*

I wept for Clayton, for having nearly lost him. I wept for the relief of holding him again now, safe and healthy and returned to us.

And I shed the tears I'd needed to shed for so long—for Homer, so that I could finally let him go.

Homer may have been the blind one, but I'd been the one who couldn't see. I had tended to dismiss Clayton's simplicity—the ease with which he found joy in absolutely everything around him—as simple-mindedness. I had thought it incompatible with depth of feeling. Sometimes (it shamed me to admit), I'd wondered if, perhaps, Clayton wasn't very *smart*.

But Clayton knew things that I didn't know—things, I realized, that Homer had known also. Perhaps that was why Clayton had clung so fast to Homer from his first day in our family, refusing to leave Homer's side even for a moment, not even at the end.

Clayton was always happy because happiness was an essential pre-condition of his life. Everybody wants happiness, and everybody tries to capture and hold it, and everybody feels the emptiness when it's gone. But Clayton spun everyday life into happiness—all of it, even the bowl of food that might not be his favorite flavor, or the unpleasantness of shots at the vet's office—the way trees turn sunlight into food, without thinking, without any deep philosophy, but as a reflexive action, simply because without it, they can't live.

In this, he was infinitely lucky.

When Homer left us, it was the first time in Clayton's short life something had happened that he couldn't spin into happiness, and he had despaired. But now, returning home after the three days in a cold, impersonal hospital, feeling loving arms around him, feeling healthy after days of being sick, he was happy once again.

I may have understood that his happiness was only the flip side of his sadness, that it only existed *because* of that sadness—but all Clayton knew was that he was happy, now, in this moment. Happy and loved. And that was enough.

Much like Homer had taught me things about life—things so simple that I should have figured them out on my own, yet might never have without him—Clayton was teaching me something now. I learned from him that happiness sometimes leaves, but that it does come back—even if it comes in a different form than the one you've lost. Loss wasn't scorched earth. It was a clay from which good things could grow—things that were strange and different from what had come before, things it might never have even occurred to you to want, but things you couldn't bear to part with once you had them.

Even if you knew you'd only gained those things by losing others that you'd have killed and died to keep forever.

THESE ARE ALL fine, lofty-sounding ideas. But for me—for me, personally—they form the very real substance of my everyday life. At the time of Homer's death, his Facebook page had roughly thirteen thousand followers. Today, only two years later, that number is nearly 750,000 and counting. Having such a large audience isn't just a "cool" thing. It's a mighty thing. Shelters write to me about special-needs animals who've been with them for years, who they can't find homes for, and Homer's community gets the word out and finds them homes within days, making way for new rescues and additional lives to be saved. "Homer's Heroes" have raised hundreds of thousands of dollars to save the lives of animals in the wake of disasters both large and small across the globe. Everything from earthquakes and tsunamis to hoarding situations, or fires at shelters so tiny and volunteer-run that they don't have a single official employee. In July of this year alone, Homer's Heroes raised over forty thousand dollars to save animals in Nepal, cats being hoarded in West Virginia who stood in danger of being destroyed, and lions on a wildlife preserve in Africa. All of the money comes from small, individual donations, and one hundred percent of the funds go directly to those for whom the funds were raised.

People share their own rescue stories on Homer's page, rescues that occur in quiet, out-of-the-way places against seemingly impossible odds. Stories that inspire others to try a little harder, to save a life they might not have thought could be saved, to give a chance to an animal whose chances might otherwise have appeared exhausted.

The greatest gift Homer left me with when he left me for good was fresh evidence every day—every single day—of the innate goodness of most people, even when news headlines make it far too easy to conclude otherwise.

In a very literal way, Homer's passing brought life in its wake. There are countless animals alive today because of Homer's loss, and the community that grew and flourished from our shared grief—which doesn't make it "worth it," but does assure me that even in his physical absence, Homer's spirit hasn't gone anywhere.

As I write this, Fanny is doing her best to insert her head between my hands and the keyboard, and Clayton is lying in my lap, flipped onto his back with one paw reaching up in his sleep to touch my face. It's a gesture that's become everyday for us, but one that never fails to knock me out anew with all the profound trust and serenity it implies.

Clayton and I might never have found each other if we hadn't lost Homer. And as much as I know that if I could wave a magic wand and undo Homer's death, I would do so in a heartbeat—in a nanosecond—I also know that I would never trade any of the things I have in my life today because I loved Homer, and also because I lost him.

Not for worlds.

GWEN COOPER is the New York Times bestselling author of the memoir *Homer's Odyssey: A Fearless Feline Tale, or How I Learned About Love and Life with a Blind Wonder Cat*; the novels *Love Saves the Day* and *Diary of a South Beach Party Girl*; and the crowd-sourced collection of cat selfies, *Kittenish*, 100% of the proceeds from which were donated to support animal rescue in Nepal following the 2015 earthquake. She is a frequent speaker at shelter fundraisers and donates 10% of her royalties from *Homer's Odyssey* to organizations that serve abused, abandoned, and disabled animals. She also manages Homer's ongoing social-media community, which reaches nearly two million cat enthusiasts and rescuers around the world each day.

Gwen lives in Manhattan with her husband, Laurence. She also lives with her two perfect cats--Clayton the Tripod and his littermate, Fanny--who aren't impressed with any of it.

60437365R00066

Made in the USA
Lexington, KY
07 February 2017